Cheers! 2019 Casey

ART OF THE
GARNISH

100+ Cocktails Finished With Style

CIDER MILL
PRESS

BOOK
PUBLISHERS
KENNEBUNKPORT, MAINE

13-Digit ISBN: 978-1604336696
10-Digit ISBN: 1604336692

This book may be ordered by mail from the publisher. Please include $5.99 for postage and handling. Please support your local bookselle first!

Books published by Cider Mill Press Book Publishers are available at special discounts for bulk purchases in the United States by corporations, institutions, and other organizations. For more information, please contact the publisher.

Cider Mill Press Book Publishers
"Where good books are ready for press"
PO Box 454
12 Spring Street
Kennebunkport, Maine 04046

Visit us online! www.cidermillpress.com

Typography: Corky, Fairfield LH, Handle Oldstyle, ITC Avant Garde Gothic, The Mix

Printed in China

1 2 3 4 5 6 7 8 9 0

First Edition

CONTENTS

INTRODUCTION

Mother Nature loves a party. How else to explain the alchemy that transforms all kinds of plants into elixirs, love potions, and brews?

Since getting booted from Eden for tasting that forbidden fruit, we've been concocting ever more creative ways to use fruits, as well as herbs, flowers, vegetables, and spices, to divine a "liquid paradise"— a cocktail—that will raise our spirits, perhaps providing a portal back to that idyllic garden.

The stories associated with the creation of classic cocktails—many of which brand themselves as being the "nectar of the gods"—are part of their seductiveness. Most spirits were first promoted as healthful tonics, and the herbs, roots, and flowers they utilized did promote healing (and still do). Over time, though, the beverages pivoted from medicinal remedies to spirited ways to celebrate.

At their best, the history of a particular cocktail combines information about its ingredients and its pedigree. Consider the Jazz Age, when Prohibition could not contain the momentum of the Roaring Twenties, and bathtubs filled with gin and champagne fueled the swoon-worthy parties and fabulous speakeasies the era is famed for.

As in a fairy tale, the cocktail slept for a decade or two. Then a cocktail renaissance came about, with boozy drinks socking it to us during the Swinging Sixties.

Then, the contemporary locavore revolution lifted "cocktail culture" to dizzying heights. In recognition of this elevated state, the James Beard Foundation introduced the Outstanding Bar Program category in 2012 "in recognition of the artisanal creations using seasonal, homegrown herbs, produce and ingredients."

Craft cocktails are now seen as unique to place, country, people, season, holiday, or event; they elicit a memory and enhance the enjoyment of entertaining. Drinks are ritual, marking sporting events such as the Kentucky Derby and cultural or religious celebrations like Mardi Gras and Christmas. Cocktails make an occasion. And the bar, serving as the altar, takes priority at nearly every event.

Consider the fierce colors present in a particularly pretty cocktail: sunset reds and oranges, cherry-blossom pinks, Caribbean emeralds, and the Côte d'Azur's intoxicating lavender. These shades serve as an ornament, elevating both the events they accompany and our memories of them.

And then there are the limitless possibilities offered by a garnish. A drink can be adorned with actual jewels (brooches, pins, clip-on earrings, or old tie tacks) or the more outré creations dreamed up by star mixologists: fire, crystals, and air.

Our connection to a particular cocktail can prove unshakable—James Bond's passion for his Martini is legendary, and some of us believe the character and style of what we drink mirrors our essence. "Bourbon with ginger and a twist, please,"

conjures that strong, smoky type. "A Cosmopolitan straight up," accompanied by a wink, suggests a playful flirt. Yet there are just as many who imbibe with caprice, whose desires shift with the season, location, occasion, or time of day.

And the garnishes are changing fashions, too—what's fresh at the farmers market or growing in the garden can add new wrinkles to our old standbys.

Cocktail culture would decree that a bartender know how to use no less than a baker's dozen of glassware, not to mention the more curious skull-shaped vessels and coconut shells. To add to the fashionable fun, a well-stocked home bar should feature far more than the standard pitcher, muddler, strainer, juicer, ice bucket, and shaker. It should also come with a treasure chest of accessories to help

you customize the drinks you serve: coasters, napkins, straws, swizzle sticks, toothpicks, and glass charms.

Cocktails have their own form, metrics, and language: there are jiggers, ponies, and shots; they are straight up, neat, or dirty, on the rocks, shaken, or stirred; there's a chaser, a split, top-shelf, and tiki.

And cocktail culture has influenced everyday conversation: you can be a "straight shooter" who uses the sayings "down the hatch," "washing it down," and "highball" (the last from the railway term for "signal to proceed," communicated by lifting a ball).

We all know the person dispensing drinks from behind a bar is called a bartender, but did you know a clumsy bartender is called a "shoemaker" or that a quick and capable one is a "mechanic"?

Clearly, cocktails are potent—they have power and influence, often acting as social arbiters. They not only possess their own times of day—cocktail hour, happy hour, and the morning after—there's also special places where we commune with cocktails, entire spaces devoted to this intimate relationship: the liquor cabinet, the cocktail lounge, the bar, and the tiki hut.

While society's devotion to cocktail culture is clear, the origin of the moniker "cocktail" remains shrouded in mystery. The first published reference to the cocktail appears in the *Farmer's Cabinet* in 1803, but the source of that reference is a bit muddled.

A few possible origins of the term "cocktail":

- ✦ It refers to the use of a rooster's, or cock's, tail as a drink garnish during the Colonial era.
- ✦ It's an allusion to an old bartending practice of stirring drinks with a feather.
- ✦ It was derived from *coquetier*, the French word for "eggcup,"

in New Orleans around the turn of the nineteenth century.

✦ A theory furthered by the shared French and American love of cocktails proposes that *coquetier* was coined as a term to describe mixed drinks in France's Bordeaux region after the concept had been imported by French officers returning from the American Revolution.

✦ The term could be a variation on *Xochitl*, the name of a legendary queen in Mexico as well as an Aztec word meaning "flower."

✦ It may also derive from "cockale," a mixture of spirits and bitters fed to fighting cocks; spectators would toast the cock with the most feathers left in his tail at the end of the fight.

Garnishes and cocktails have long been inextricably linked, with the former providing the crucial finishing touch that a memorable libation requires.

In putting together *Art of the Garnish*, I started to think of it as the embodiment of a great cocktail party. In addition to the inspired garnishes and cocktails of my own formulation, I am honored and privileged to have as my guests some of the world's best mixologists, bartenders, and brands, including Patrón, Chandon, Macchu Pisco, and Möet Hennessy. As the hostess of this party, I was fortunate to be able to select from a spectacular talent pool in order to gather a mix of suave gentlemen, accomplished women, explorers, swashbucklers, and artists. Their creativity in designing drinks and garnishes is nothing short of breathtaking. Their recipes made my pulse quicken and caused me to exclaim, "How'd they come up with that?" Their stories of how, and why, they did make their inventions even more intriguing.

Art of the Garnish elevates the art of the cocktail. It gilds the lily—adding an aesthetic component that transforms the process of crafting cocktails into theater.

So cheers to those who aren't afraid to flirt with fresh, seasonal ingredients, to craft their own bitters, infusions, and syrups, and to embellish their libations with pristine garnishes.

Eden is ever closer.

HERBS AND SPICES

An emphasis on quality ingredients has elevated bartending to an art, a dynamic arena where homegrown, hard-to-find, and handcrafted elements are used to reinvigorate classic cocktails and create innovative, sophisticated novelties.

Herbs—savory and aromatic plant leaves—and spices work especially well as a garnish adorning the glass and the tablescape, particularly when paired with artisanal spirits, amari, apéritifs, and digestifs.

Aromatic herbs and spices derived from tree bark, roots, and other sources have long been valued for their medicinal properties. Many of the tonics and bitters that line a top-tier bar today got their start in an apothecary.

If there's one category of garnish that's taken the passion for mixology to the next level, herbs and spices surely take the crown. Most herbs require little more than a slap to awaken their flavor. Seriously! A good whack releases or activates the aroma of an herb. You can rub, crush, and muddle them, too—and the same goes for spices.

That mint leaf floating in your Mojito isn't just there to look pretty; think of it as a fragrant flirtation,

enticing your nose and taste buds before you even take a sip. Charring rosemary expresses the oils and lends a piney, smoky quality to a drink, evoking images of cozy evenings by the fire while the snow falls outside.

These earthy elements add aromatic, musky, sweet, or bitter notes that amplify the seasonal qualities of a particular cocktail. The array of herbs and spices can seem dizzying, but if you remember to keep it simple and allow their

essence to shine, your cocktails will follow suit.

OVERVIEW OF HERBS AND SPICES

There are as many herbs and spices as there are drinks, from achiote (nutty, sweet, and musky) to wormwood (a savory, bitter herb used to flavor absinthe and various love potions).

The best herbs and spices are fresh, coming either from your garden or from the farmers market. If you cultivate a cocktail herb garden, foraging for fresh ingredients will be as close as your windowsill or backyard. Herbs are perhaps the easiest plants to grow, whether you're starting from seed or buying ready-to-pot plants. An herb garden is also a great place to recycle your well-worn, alcohol-related wares. Use old cocktail shakers or glasses for pots, rehabilitate swizzle sticks as stakes, and put wine corks down as mulch.

Mint is one of the easiest herbs to grow. Long used to aid digestion or soothe an upset stomach, mint is also the key ingredient in one of the most enduring mixed drinks: the Julep. The possibilities for this herb don't stop at peppermint and spearmint; there's also orange, rose, pineapple, chocolate, and apple mints to add panache to your chosen painkiller.

Beyond mint, you'll want to consider these herbal stalwarts as well: rosemary, lavender, tarragon,

sage, and basil. And there are plenty of unusual options at the vanguard of the craft-cocktail renaissance. Angelica ("herb of the angels") is a member of the parsley family. Once thought to be a remedy against witchcraft, poison, and plague, it has an earthy flavor with notes of anise and juniper, and the flowers are honey-like. Bergamot's leaves possess a citrusy taste with spicy notes, and so do its delicate flowers. Agastache (a licorice-smelling herb), verbena, and shiso may be off the beaten path, but are all worthy garnishes due to their unique fragrance, taste, and attractiveness.

If you're looking for something other than horseradish to spice up your Bloody Mary, give lovage, a perennial heirloom herb, a try. Traditionally used to prevent kidney stones and dehydration, its flavor and aroma bring to mind an amped-up celery. Lovage is also great for making teas or syrups that can enrich other cocktails. Aside from the standbys mentioned above, anise hyssop and cilantro are also great options in infusions.

The universally loved cinnamon comes from the bark of a tree commonly grown in tropical climates. When crushed, it possesses a sweet fragrance that is at the heart of so many comforting recipes. You can also use cinnamon sticks to garnish hot and cold beverages or to serve as a swizzle stick or straw. When crushed and sprinkled on a cocktail, particularly when accompanying an orange wheel or chocolate shavings, cinnamon adds unmatched savor.

The Dutch "architecture aromatique" firm Koppert Cress provides expert guidance in taking your cocktail game up a sprig or two. This resource to top-tier chefs and mixologists the world over offers a stunning kaleidoscope of exquisite flowers, herbs, and microgreens to be

utilized as condiments and garnishes. Its Dulce Buttons, for example, are pretty green-and-white flowers that manage to be very sweet while also carrying the famous freshness of mint. Koppert Cress claims its Szechuan Button flower is downright electric, as the taste starts with "a Champagne-like sensation at the top of the tongue [before] moving on around the mouth in a kind of 'Pop Rocks' sensation."

When marrying garnishes and cocktail flavors, a tasty and fun way to add a finishing touch is to look at herbs and fruits that have something in common and can be naturally wedded. For example, cucumber, apple, cherry, watermelon, and strawberry are a natural pairing with rose-infused spirits, by and large, because they are all in the same plant family (*rosaceae*). Not such a curious surprise, then, that their flavors pair up like siblings playing peek-a-boo in a cocktail composition. Other go-to combations are cardamom with ginger, cinnamon, vanilla, or thyme.

HARVESTING THE GARNISH

Just as you build your meals around what ingredients are in season, your cocktail garnishes should reflect the time of the year.

Chef Claudia Fleming's rule—"If it's *never* going to grow in your garden, then purchase"—applies to things like black pepper, cinnamon, cardamom, star anise, and turmeric for folks in the northern hemisphere. Otherwise, use herbs and spices that are in season, whether harvested straight from your garden or procured at the farmers market. While it's ideal to grow your own herbs, you should always harvest them early in the morning, as close to serving time as possible, before the sun begins to cook the herbs' essential oils.

Cutting an herb's leaves and stems is a fun, easy, and elegant way to harvest the garnish. In fact, cutting or pruning is healthier for the plant, and will provide you with plenty of happy hours.

For basil, mint, tarragon, and shiso, snip the stem just above where two leaves are growing. Cut the entire stalk for parsley, lavender, chives, and rosemary.

When cutting sage, dill, and cilantro, start from the top down; pick the leaves off or run your fingers down the stalk to remove them. Once you've got what you need, slap the herbs to release their aromatic oils.

HOW TO STORE

Wash and drain the fresh herbs or spices on damp paper towels or wax paper and store in an airtight container in the refrigerator or in a cool place until cocktail hour.

You can also freeze fresh herbs and spices in ice cubes for frozen, iced, or "out-of-season" drinks, such as a mojito in March!

Drying is another useful form of preservation. After washing and drying the herbs, tie their roots and hang them in a well-lit area until they are dry and crumbly to the touch, approximately 1 week. Once they are dry, store in airtight containers in a cool, dry place.

MUDDLING AND CRUSHING

Muddling herbs is the best method to release their essential oils. Using a muddler made of unvarnished wood, place the washed leaves in a cocktail shaker or mixing glass, and press down while making a few gentle twists to bruise the herbs and release their fragrance. Add the cocktail's other ingredients and mix according to the recipe. You can also use your hands to crush the herbs. If you're looking for an added bit of flair, use an herb grinder to crush the fresh herbs into a paste and rim the cocktail glass with it, or sprinkle on the drink's foam for a decorative touch.

These same techniques and approaches will work for spices; the original cocktail garnish was perhaps freshly grated nutmeg.

HERBAL DISPLAY GARNISHES

Herbs' ability to amplify a fragrance and intoxicate the nose means that there is no shortage of ways to use them as garnishes.

You can use mini clothespins (which are available in themed and holiday variations) to attach herbs to the glass's rim. This works especially well with delicate herbs such as tarragon and orange thyme (which look glorious with Aperol-based cocktails).

You can bunch lavender, sage, rose, and other fragrant herbs in a kind of nosegay that takes its cue from Victorians' use of nosegays to send secret messages: roses signal love, while a yellow garnish says friendship, coral says sympathy, and orange says desire.

Floating a leaf, sprig, or bud in a drink is a lovely, simple indulgence. Rosemary, lavender, and tarragon are particularly charming when viewed from a side angle.

Rim a glass with dried herbs, herb-infused salts or sugars, herbal syrup, or balsamic vinegar infused with herbs (I especially love basil-infused balsamics) for a bit of cocktail couture. When paired with an edible flower afloat in the glass, the result is nothing short of runway-worthy.

HERBAL BITTERS

You can readily create your own artisanal bitters and herbal tinctures from botanicals—or source them from a plethora of award-winning purveyors, including Modern Bar Cart, Hella Cocktail Co., Regan's, Fee Brothers, and the classics Peychaud's and Angostura.

HOW TO INFUSE SPIRITS WITH HERBS AND SPICES

Vodka is the drink world's shape-shifter; it blends well with almost anything. Tequila, rum, and gin are versatile spirits as well. Combine the spirit with crushed or muddled herbs and spices, such as ginger, cilantro, or angelica, and store in a cool, dark place until the taste is to your liking.

When you're using these infused spirits in cocktails, look for tastes that complement each other, like angelica with orange, rhubarb, or strawberry; anise hyssop with blueberry, peach, or raspberry; basil with lime, mint, or cinnamon; or cilantro with coconut, lemon, or mint.

SYRUPS

There's a good reason why the best bars are stocked with an array of flavored syrups: they boost the flavors of fresh, seasonal ingredients to add a touch of sophistication and nuance to a cocktail. Syrups are also a great flavoring agent for still or sparkling water.

The basis of any cocktail syrup is simple syrup, which is aptly named because it is, well, simple to make. It requires only two ingredients: water and sugar, in equal proportions. Heat up the water, add the sugar, and stir, while continuing to cook, until the sugar has dissolved. Once dissolved, add a herb or spice, stir to combine, and let the mixture cool for a few hours. Strain out the flavoring component and store in the refrigerator for up to 1 month to ensure a fresh cocktail adventure.

MEDITERRANEAN SUNRISE

Ouzo is thought of as an apéritif and usually served on the rocks with a lemon twist. Many claim drinking ouzo is an art, but don't be intimidated. Sipping is the simple key to unlocking the flavor in this potent anise-flavored spirit.

1 to 1¹/₂ cups orange (or other fruit) juice

1¹/₂ oz. ouzo

1¹/₂ oz. tequila

a few dashes of peach bitters or grenadine

Pour the juice into a tall glass over ice, add the ouzo and tequila, and top with the bitters or grenadine.

FINISHING TOUCHES
Garnish with skewered wedges of fruit and a piece of red licorice. The flavor of the licorice not only complements ouzo's anise flavor, it makes for pretty and fun presentation. Use a red glass to boost the cocktail's color, and set it off with red-and-white or blue-and-white cocktail napkins.

Cocktails of the World

"This is *uso Massalia,* my friends." According to legend, this statement was made by an Ottoman consul upon tasting the local drink while touring the commercial docks of nineteenth-century Thessaly, in Greece. He must have been at a loss for words because in front of him was a shipment of silkworm cocoons bound for Marseille stamped with the Italian label *uso Massalia*—meaning "of the highest quality." Nevertheless, the name *uso,* or *ouzo,* stuck. Ouzo has been long regarded as a symbol of Greek culture—of the highest quality, of course!

RED JUBILEE

This fiery red drink's garnish of star anise and cocktail cherry is sure to spice up your fortune. When asked about his formulation, Jordan wrote, "The use of Chinese five-spice in the cocktail makes it unique. Star anise is a key ingredient in Chinese five-spice. This drink was created for Chinese New Year, so all the elements you see in the background are themed for good luck."

Jordan Bushell, national brand ambassador for Hennessy

---

2 oz. Hennessy V.S.O.P Privilège

3/4 oz. fresh lemon juice

3/4 oz. simple syrup

1/4 teaspoon Chinese five-spice powder

5 dashes of Peychaud's Bitters

Combine all ingredients in a cocktail shaker filled with ice, shake until chilled, and strain into an Old Fashioned glass containing fresh ice.

FINISHING TOUCHES
Garnish with star anise and a Luxardo maraschino cherry.

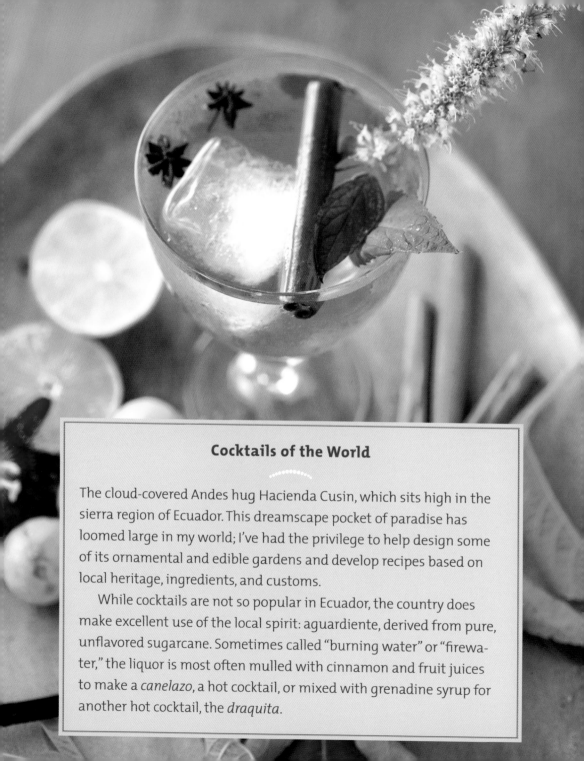

Cocktails of the World

The cloud-covered Andes hug Hacienda Cusin, which sits high in the sierra region of Ecuador. This dreamscape pocket of paradise has loomed large in my world; I've had the privilege to help design some of its ornamental and edible gardens and develop recipes based on local heritage, ingredients, and customs.

While cocktails are not so popular in Ecuador, the country does make excellent use of the local spirit: aguardiente, derived from pure, unflavored sugarcane. Sometimes called "burning water" or "firewater," the liquor is most often mulled with cinnamon and fruit juices to make a *canelazo*, a hot cocktail, or mixed with grenadine syrup for another hot cocktail, the *draquita*.

HUMMINGBIRD-CUSIN COCKTAIL

The Hacienda Cusin, a hotel in Ecuador that has been operating since the early seventeenth century, makes a special welcome drink using their artisanal punta, a local variant of aguardiente and just-picked herbs. My remix is named for the buzzing, darting jewel of a bird that seems to be everywhere at Hacienda Cusin.

2 to 3 cinnamon sticks

blooms or heads from 2 stems of amaranth

bouquet of anise or sweet cumin

1½ oz. *punta* or aguardiente (sugar cane liquor)

1 barspoon of fresh lemon juice

sugar or honey, to taste

Steep the cinnamon, amaranth, and anise or sweet cumin in warm water for a few minutes.

Strain the tea into a Irish coffee glass or goblet, add the liquor, lemon juice, and sugar or honey, and stir.

FINISHING TOUCHES
Garnish with edible flowers, or float a star anise in the drink and add another cinnamon stick.

VARIATION
Hacienda Cusin is known for its colorful juices made from just-picked orange, naranjilla, tomate de árbol, pineapple, and mora (a kind of raspberry). For a cold variation on this cocktail, add the ingredients (without the sugar or honey) to fresh fruit pureed with simple syrup and pour over ice.

FIZZY FRUIT SPLASH

This refreshing, smoothie-like drink relies on local, seasonal fresh fruits and herbs. An edible flower garnish adds a touch of summer romance. This recipe makes four servings.

20 to 25 seasonal berries

juice of 6 large lemons

water, as needed

25 lemon basil leaves

3 oz. simple syrup

24 oz. club soda

Wash the fruit and place it in the blender with the juice from 2 lemons and a few tablespoons of water, just enough to get the fruit to puree. Puree until smooth and set aside.

Place ice in a cocktail shaker, add the remaining lemon juice and the basil leaves, and shake well for 30 seconds to release the aromatics from the basil.

Strain the infused lemon juice into the fruit puree, add the simple syrup, and stir to incorporate.

Fill highball glasses with ice and add one-quarter of the puree to each glass.

Top each glass with the club soda.

FINISHING TOUCHES
Garnish each glass with a sprig of lemon basil. For a true Cusin experience, drop edible fuchsia blossoms and/or passionflowers into the glass.

Passionflower fruit can also be used in this cocktail. It is known for its calming properties and is said to be an aphrodisiac, while fuchsia is used to soothe sore throats and to strengthen the voice. All the more reason to say, "I'll have another Fizzy Fruit Splash, please!"

HI-POTION

The aromatic layering in this cocktail is the key to its unique flavor. What this cocktail lacks in ABV, it more than makes up for in subtlety and nuance.

Jessica Wohlers, general manager and mixologist at Leyenda, Brooklyn

1 oz. shochu

1 ½ oz. Cocchi Americano

1 oz. Manzanilla sherry

Place all of the ingredients in a mixing glass filled with ice and stir until chilled.

Strain into a coupe.

FINISHING TOUCHES
Garnish with a spritz of oregano hydrosol (an essential oil that imparts the plant's scent) and an orange twist. The oils in the twist add a touch of sweetness to the cocktail, while the oregano adds a pleasant layer to the drink's nose.

SWEATER WEATHER

"The Sweater Weather was created in the fall with the intention of merging two of my favorite cocktails: the Hot Toddy and the Dark and Stormy," says cocktail artist Jessica Wohlers. While the drink is served over ice, the heat from the rye whiskey and the clove echoes the flavors of the Hot Toddy, and the rum and ginger mimic the Dark and Stormy.

Jessica Wohlers, general manager and mixologist at Leyenda, Brooklyn

1¹/₂ oz. El Dorado 12-Year-Old rum

³/₄ oz. Rittenhouse Straight Rye Whiskey

¹/₂ oz. Cointreau

¹/₂ oz. ginger syrup

³/₄ oz. fresh lemon juice

Place all of the ingredients in a cocktail shaker filled with ice and shake vigorously.

Strain over ice into a double Old Fashioned glass.

FINISHING TOUCHES

Garnish with a twist of lemon and a whole clove.

For ginger syrup: Add a peeled 1-inch piece of ginger to a standard simple syrup after the sugar has dissolved. Let cool, strain, and store in an airtight container.

SPICE WHISPERER GARNISHES

Lior Lev Sercarz is the chef, spice blender, and owner of La Boîte, a biscuits and spices shop in New York City. He has earned a reputation as the "Spice Whisperer" for his ability to take the guesswork out of creating spice blends. His curated collection recaptures the magic and excitement that sent European explorers all over the globe in search of spices in the fifteenth, sixteenth, and seventeenth centuries.

Spice Cocktail Suggestions:

✦ Create artisanal ice cubes by adding individual spices or spice blends—handcrafted or La Boîte blends—to water before freezing. In addition to the luscious visual of spices floating in a glass, you will imbue the drink with a sparkling élan. As the drink is sipped and the ice melts, the spices leave an artful remnant in the bottom of the glass. How dreamy is Orchidea N. 34 with a blend of Sichuan pepper, lime, and orchid root, or Lula N. 41 with seaweed, coriander, fennel seeds, and salt?

✦ For added drama, use ground spices or blends on the edge of your glass instead of a traditional sugar or salt rim. Sheba N. 40, Lior's powerful interpretation of Ethiopia's traditional berbere (a blend of non-native spices, including paprika, ginger, and cumin), can stand up to a variety of cocktails, particularly those featuring spicy spirits, like tequila, Ancho Reyes, or chile liqueur. The same goes for Penang N. 31, with its sweet chilies, onion, and turmeric, and Shabazi N. 38, with green chilies, parsley, and coriander. And don't overlook Amber N. 2 and its ancho, annatto, and mace.

✦ Sprinkle spices on fruit or vegetable garnishes to enhance the flavor and add to a drink's complexity. Kibbeh N. 15 combines parsley, garlic, and cumin, making it ideal on the celery stalk in a Bloody Mary.

✦ Create your own unique infused spirits or simple syrups by infusing them with spices. Galil N. 13 boasts verbena, white cardamom, and sage; Sri Lanka N. 14 features cinnamon and star anise; Noga N. 17 has lemongrass, ginger, and palm sugar. All three blends work well with vodka and other neutral spirits as well as a limitless variety of simple syrups.

✦ Muddle whole spices while constructing a cocktail to obtain a pungent, spicy flavor.

PINK CRUSH

This sparkling cocktail is so seductive that you just might end up blushing. The subtle, spicy sweetness of pink peppercorn syrup combines with the tanginess of grapefruit. Top that dynamic duo with Chandon's favorite rosé and you'll be smitten.

Courtesy of Chandon

2 oz. grapefruit juice

1/2 oz. pink peppercorn syrup

2 oz. Chandon Rosé

Pour the grapefruit juice and syrup into an Old Fashioned glass and stir to combine.

Add ice and top with the rosé.

FINISHING TOUCHES
Sprinkle 1/2 teaspoon of crushed pink peppercorns on top.

For pink peppercorn syrup: Add 2 teaspoons pink peppercorns, 1/2 cup water, and 1/2 cup sugar to a saucepan and bring to a boil. Remove from heat and let cool for at least 30 minutes. Strain and store in an airtight container.

PINK CHANDY

"A little bit naughty and a little bit nice" describes the mix of sweet and spice in this muscular, bubbly cocktail.

Courtesy of Chandon

2 oz. pink lemonade

2 dashes of Fee Brothers Lemon Bitters

3 oz. Chandon Rosé

Pour the lemonade into an Old Fashioned glass containing ice, or into a champagne flute with no ice.

Add the bitters and top with the rosé.

FINISHING TOUCHES
Drop a slice of jalapeño pepper into the drink.

HEART OF GOLD

Gustav Klimt's The Kiss *is about love, lust, and gold. In that painting, and in this cocktail, the artful use of gold leaf proves transformative.*

1/2 oz. Goldschläger cinnamon schnapps

3/4 to 1 oz. cold ginger beer (homemade or artisanal)

2 to 3 dashes of Fee Brothers Cherry Bitters

GOLD WAFER COTTON CANDY
2 cups granulated sugar

1/2 cup water

1/2 cup corn syrup

Fill a goblet with ice cubes.

Place all of the ingredients in a cocktail shaker filled with ice and shake vigorously.

Remove ice from the goblet and strain the cocktail into it.

FINISHING TOUCHES
Garnish with crystallized ginger, or use a gold pin to affix an orange rind studded with cloves onto the glass. You can also go all in on the gold theme and spin some gold-tinged cotton candy on a lollipop stick. Intrigued? Just look below.

GOLD WAFER COTTON CANDY
Place the sugar, water, and corn syrup in a saucepan and cook, while stirring, over medium-high heat until the sugar dissolves.

Cover and boil for 2 to 3 minutes, then remove the lid and stir occasionally.

As soon as the mixture reaches 310°F (make sure it doesn't burn toward the end), remove from heat and place the saucepan in ice water to stop the cooking process. Let stand for 1 to 2 minutes.

Create a scaffold to hang the sugar on: cover wooden spoons (3 or 4) with nonstick cooking spray, and arrange on parchment paper.

Stir the cooled sugar with a fork. Flick it, moving back and forth, over your scaffold, so that it starts to resemble wool or a nest.

Mold the spun sugar into wafers—they will be oddly shaped, not perfectly round. Take a lollipop stick and wrap the spun sugar around the stick, as you would see with a cotton candy machine.

CITY OF GOLD

Mixologist Isaac Morrison visited the region of Peru where the spirit pisco is made, staying in the otherworldly oasis of Huacachina. Looking at the village from the dunes at sunset, he felt as though he'd found a lost city. Locals told him that you can still find gold in the Lake of Huacachina—and that everyone who has tried eventually lost their mind.

Isaac Morrison, drink consultant at Dash Concept

⅓ teaspoon aji pepper powder

⅔ teaspoon caster sugar

1 lemon wedge

¼ oz. Solbeso cacao liqueur

1 oz. pisco (Macchu Pisco is recommended)

½ oz. apricot liqueur

¼ oz. fresh lemon juice

1½ oz. cava or prosecco

Combine the aji pepper powder and caster sugar in a saucer.

Run the lemon wedge halfway around the rim of a chilled coupette. Dip the wet part of the rim into the aji-and-sugar mixture. Leave the other half as is.

Place all of the remaining cocktail ingredients, except for the cava or prosecco, in a mixing glass filled with ice and stir for 20 seconds.

Strain into the rimmed glass and top with the sparkling wine.

FINISHING TOUCHES
Garnish with a fancy orange twist.

DON'T WORRY ABOUT ERIK

This drink was a collaboration between Fabiano and a colleague named Erik, who started as a miserable and cheeky bar steward but soon became infected by the inspirational spirit of the bar. Erik's stock phrase when being complimented is, "Don't worry about me," so they named this calming drink after him.

Fabiano Latham, beverage director for Chotto Matte, London

1 cup Nikkei orgeat (see below)

1 1/2 oz. Macchu Pisco

2/3 oz. fresh lime juice

1 oz. pineapple juice

2/3 oz. egg white

splash of soda water

Add all of the ingredients, except for the soda water, to a cocktail shaker with no ice and dry shake.

Add ice to the shaker and shake vigorously.

Strain the cocktail, discard the ice, and return the cocktail to the shaker. Dry shake for 10 seconds.

Pour into a small, chilled highball glass and top with the splash of soda water.

FINISHING TOUCHES
Season the foam with a few drops of ají amarillo–infused mezcal (see below).

For Nikkei orgeat: Combine 1 1/4 cup white sugar, 1/2 cup unsweetened almond milk, 3 1/2 oz. nigori sake (or preferred sake), 1 teaspoon almond extract, and 3 oz. cognac and mix well. Pour into a bottle and refrigerate.

For ají amarillo–infused mezcal: Steep 2 ají amarillo peppers (aka Peruvian yellow chilies) in 3 1/2 oz. mezcal for at least 12 hours.

CURIOUS GEORGE NO. 2

"Because the cocktail contains banana liqueur, I thought it would be fun to play off the Curious George monkey character," noted Williams. "And the No. 2 reference is founded on my belief that drink names pretty much come in three varieties. . . . A No. 2 leads you to believe that there was a No. 1."

KJ Williams, bartender at Flatiron Lounge, New York

1¹/₂ oz. Avuá Cachaça Prata

³/₄ oz. Giffard Banane du Brésil

¹/₂ oz. fresh lemon juice

¹/₂ oz. Fireball Cinnamon Whisky

Place all of the ingredients in a cocktail shaker containing 2 ice cubes and briefly shake.

Strain into a double Old Fashioned glass containing pellet ice that has been formed into a kind of snow cone.

FINISHING TOUCHES
Top with a dusting of Vietnamese cinnamon and dehydrated banana chips.

ABSINTHE-MINDED COCKTAIL

Aromatic mint leaves on top of this cocktail allow you to "drink in" the fresh smell as you lift the glass to your lips. The orange oil echoes the citrusy elements of the gin. "A good garnish first attracts the drinker with its beauty and charm, then it adds to the taste, mirroring its flavors," says Williams.

KJ Williams, bartender at Flatiron Lounge, New York

Herbsaint anise-flavored liqueur, to rinse

2 oz. Plymouth gin

3/4 oz. fresh lime juice

3/4 oz. Velvet Falernum

Place the Herbsaint in a coupe, swirl to coat, and discard the excess.

Place the remaining ingredients in a cocktail shaker filled with ice and shake vigorously.

Double-strain into the coupe.

FINISHING TOUCHES
Place a slapped mint leaf on the surface of the drink and then add an orange twist with pointed ends.

ROOTING FOR LOVE

Amaro Averna is an Italian botanical curative made from a recipe that dates back to 1868. It is a digestive, or digestivo, that is part of a group of liqueurs known collectively as amari. The word refers to their shared bitterness, which is derived from quinine. Averna is sweet and thick, and its gentle herbal bite is good for sipping, but ideal when mixed with prosecco.

4 oz. prosecco

Amaro Averna, to taste

Pour the prosecco into a champagne flute and top with Amaro Averna.

FINISHING TOUCHES
Garnish with ground star anise, and feel free to toss in a cinnamon stick.

Cocktail Presentation

The tobacco-colored liqueur invites warm-colored napkins and metallic or glass serving trays lined with a charger (patterned paper—perhaps a mahogany mosaic). Vintage cocktail coasters and an herbal potpourri set in glittering crystal will also heighten the presentation.

GINGER JALAPEÑO

Several of Valentina Carbone's cocktails have become signature drinks at London's Nobu Berkeley St. This one gets spicy with ginger liqueur, fresh basil, and a slice of jalapeño. Yowza!

Valentina Carbone, bartender at Nobu Berkeley St, London

6 fresh basil leaves

1 slice of fresh jalapeño pepper

1/2 oz. gomme syrup

1/2 oz. fresh lemon juice

2 oz. vodka

2/3 oz. ginger liqueur

Place the basil, jalapeño, and gomme syrup in a cocktail shaker, muddle, and then remove the jalapeño.

Add the remaining ingredients and ice, shake vigorously, and strain into a cocktail glass.

FINISHING TOUCHES
Lay a long, thin slice of jalapeño (or your preferred green chili pepper) across the top of the glass.

For gomme syrup: Add 1 oz. of gum arabic to 1/4 cup of near-boiling water and let stand for a few hours, until the gum arabic has dissolved and the mixture is a sticky paste. Stir until smooth. Place 1 cup sugar and 1/2 cup water in a saucepan and bring to a boil, while stirring. When the sugar is dissolved, reduce heat to low and stir in the dissolved gum arabic. Simmer, while stirring, for approximately 5 minutes, until a very thick syrup forms. Use a spoon to remove any foam from the surface and let cool. Strain into a bottle and store in the refrigerator.

ONCE UPON A TIME

Here's another of Valentina's creations, this time with the kick coming from lemongrass. The dehydrated grapefruit is another of her genius touches.

Valentina Carbone, bartender at Nobu Berkeley St, London

1 lemongrass stalk, minced, 1 piece reserved for garnish

1/2 oz. chamomile syrup

1/2 oz. fresh lemon juice

1 3/4 oz. gin

2/3 oz. bergamot liqueur

1/2 oz. grapefruit juice

Fernet-Branca, to top

Place the lemongrass and the syrup in a cocktail shaker and muddle.

Add the remaining ingredients, except for the Fernet-Branca, and ice to the shaker and shake vigorously.

Strain into a coupette or Old Fashioned glass containing an ice cube and top with the Fernet-Branca.

FINISHING TOUCHES
Muddle the reserved piece of lemongrass on the top so that it resembles a small fan. Garnish with this and a slice of dehydrated grapefruit (see below).

For chamomile syrup: Add 1 tablespoon of chamomile flowers or 2 bags of chamomile tea to a standard simple syrup after the sugar has dissolved. Let cool, strain, and store in an airtight container.

For dehydrated grapefruit: Preheat the oven to 400°F. Place slices of grapefruit on a parchment-lined baking sheet and bake in the oven until crisp, approximately 7 minutes.

CLASSIC MINT JULEP

The Mint Julep's pedigree can be traced back to the original cocktail book, How to Mix Drinks, or The Bon Vivant's Companion *by Jerry Thomas, which was published in 1862. That recipe (which features cognac in place of the whiskey that is commonly used today) called for more peach or apricot brandy, but the peach brandy of the time was not as sweet as what we have today. This adaptation accounts for that shift, whittling down the amount to create the balanced, refreshing taste this classic is known for.*

Jordan Bushell, national brand ambassador for Hennessy

12 mint leaves

2 teaspoons sugar

2 oz. Hennessy V.S

½ oz. peach or apricot brandy

Place the mint leaves in a tin Julep cup or Old Fashioned glass, add the sugar, and muddle.

Add crushed ice and pour the Hennessy and brandy over the ice.

Stir briskly until chilled and add more crushed ice.

FINISHING TOUCHES
The garnish for the drink has historically been mint. Add 2 sprigs to provide a refreshing look and a gentle yet bright aroma. You can also add an apricot or peach slice that has been dusted with powdered sugar for greater visual appeal.

CUBAN CIGAR

When Tom started to tend bar, patrons were continually asking about the heritage responsible for his last name. When he responded that his grandfather was from Cuba, they invariably asked him for a Cuban cocktail. Naturally, he started with a Mojito, which at that time was rare in the States. Over the years he's used his painterly eye for detail to refine his signature cocktail, making it the perfect complement to some of the Cuban dishes served at the restaurant. Upon seeing the elaborate garnish, guests started calling this drink "Tommy's Cuban Cigar," and the moniker has stuck.

Tom Sebazco, entrepreneur and bartender at Fitzgerald's Pub, New York

2 oz. coconut rum

1 oz. amaretto

squeeze of fresh lime juice

Place the ingredients in a cocktail shaker filled with ice and shake vigorously.

Strain into a cocktail glass.

FINISHING TOUCHES
Place a fresh cherry or Homemade Maraschino Cherry (see page 113) on each end of a cinnamon stick and then wrap a twist of lime around the cinnamon stick. As you'll see if you manage to pull off this delicate balancing act, the result resembles a cigar.

CUBAN MOJITO

The mint used in Cuban Mojitos is yerba buena, or hierba buena, which carries a more citrus-forward, earthy flavor than the spearmint that is found in much of the U.S.

Courtesy of La Bodeguita del Medio, the famous bar in Old Havana, Cuba

---

1½ teaspoons white cane sugar

⅓ oz. fresh key lime juice

2 sprigs of hierba buena

2 oz. sparkling mineral water, plus a splash

1½ oz. Bacardi Superior or Havana Club Añejo 3 Años rum

Place the sugar, key lime juice, hierba buena, and the splash of mineral water in a tall glass and muddle.

Add the remaining mineral water, 2 to 3 large ice cubes, and the rum and stir to combine.

FINISHING TOUCHES

Serve with a colorful straw and key limes, which can be floated, perched on the rim, or tattooed (see page 75).

CUBAN COCKTAILS

Havana cast a spell on me long before I ever visited: the combination of the music, the cuisine, the rum, and the mystery slowly drew me in over the years.

In 2000, I traveled there with a small group, just after Elián González captured all the headlines and a number of hearts in

America. The focus of my Cuban excursion was sustainable urban farming. After the collapsing Soviet Union stopped supporting the island, people began to starve. Ever industrious, the Cubans adapted, and urban agriculture became part of the landscape long before it appeared in the United States.

While in Havana, my friend George and I gravitated toward Ernest Hemingway's home, Finca Vigía, and the El Floridita bar, where in the 1930s, a bartender named Constante invented the frozen Daiquiri, which is why the bar's motto is "la cuna del daiquiri" (the cradle of the Daiquiri).

Eager to make up for lost time, my friend and I drank our fair share of Daiquiris—toasting to Hemingway each time, of course.

HAVANA DAIQUIRI

This beautiful drink is so popular it earned its very own glass. Refreshing, joyful, and elegant, the Daiquiri has everything you want in a classic cocktail.

Courtesy of Havana Club

---

2 teaspoons sugar

juice of ½ lime

2 sprigs of mint

3 oz. sparkling mineral water

¼ oz. Havana Club Añejo 3 Años rum

Place the sugar, lime juice, mint, and sparkling water in a mixing glass and gently muddle.

Add the rum and 4 ice cubes, stir until chilled, and strain into a Daiquiri glass.

FINISHING TOUCHES

Cut a long, swirling strip of lime peel and either place it on the rim so that it just touches the cocktail, or wrap a sprig of mint around it and skewer the pair with a cocktail pick.

You can also place a lime wedge—tattooed (see page 75) or as is—on the edge of the glass or in the cocktail.

CITRUS
BLISS

Cultures the world over have long extolled the salubrious properties of citrus fruits. Pliny the Elder noted that citrus can serve as an antidote to poison when taken in wine; in Europe, royalty sought out citrus because of its nutritional benefits; and let's not forget those "limeys," the members of the British navy who sucked on limes to ward off scurvy.

The earliest known reference to citrus peel as a cocktail garnish appears in Jerry Thomas's 1862 classic *How to Mix Drinks, or The Bon Vivant's Companion*, the first drink book published in the U.S. Thomas also recommended fruit or berries "in season when ornamentation is called for, and lemons when in need of citrus." Not long after, in 1892, William Schmidt mentioned the use of citrus and fruit in his book *The Flowing Bowl*: "lemons, oranges, the delicious pineapple, choice grapes, and strawberries, raspberries, and cherries." Limes came later.

Citrus as a garnish has more or less been codified over the years, so much so that we think a lemon twist simply must be used with a Sidecar, Sazerac, or Martini and believe that there is no substitute for a lime wedge in a cool and refreshing Gin and Tonic. And while it's true that today the most popular citrus garnishes are lemon, lime, and orange (with grapefruit "squeezing" in close behind), it's also true that yuzu, tangelo, and pummelo are contemporary versions of the exotic lemons and oranges that the earliest bartenders experimented with.

Citrus enhances a cocktail— adding fragrance, taste (both au naturel and candied), and aesthetics.

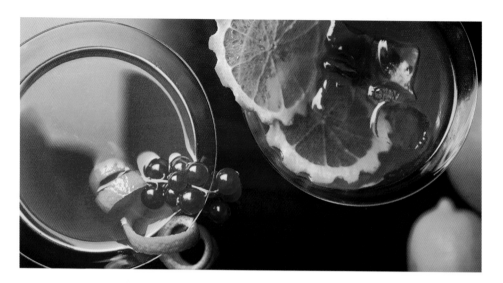

The color of citrus not only lends a cocktail a photogenic burst, it can also pull off any look: perched on the rim, threading the inside of the glass, or floating languidly on the surface of the cocktail.

The thick skin of citrus lends a theatrical element to a strip of peel, allowing it to morph into a wheel, a bow, a knot, a star, a wedge, a spiral, a tattoo, or a flower. It can evolve into various creatures—why not a cobra for the Mojito or a butterfly for your apéritif spritzer?—and shine under the intense heat of a flame.

Citrus is a member of the *Rutaceae* family of flowering plants. Their leaves are aromatic, and the flowers feature a heady fragrance designed to attract pollinators and creative cocktail enthusiasts alike. You can use every part of a citrus plant in creating garnishes, since both the flowers and the blossoms are edible.

Rubbing the rim of a glass with the citrus rind probably came about for two reasons: first is taste, as the essences of the citrus oils are expressed. Second, citrus was so rare at the time of the nascent cocktail culture that bartenders and saloon owners wanted to use every last drop. Citrus was a sign of conspicuous consumption, and they weren't about to waste any of it.

When shopping for citrus, and produce in general, it's best to go organic. Fertilizer, pesticides, and herbicides are not cocktail ingredients! Plus, organic produce provides more nutrients and antioxidants; studies note that eating organic fruits (and vegetables) increases one's antioxidant intake by up to 40 percent. Best of all, organics simply offer superior flavor, which is the most important component in every leading mixologist's alchemy.

TOOLS

In order to get garnishes that can shine under scrutiny, citrus requires specific tools and some practice to attain the proper amount of precision. Common kitchen workhorses like the paring knife, vegetable peeler, box grater, and microplane will serve you well for almost any garnish you want to construct. But in order to achieve the sophistication seen at the highest levels of mixology, you may need a few specialized tools, such as:

- ✦ Zester and Citrus Peeler: Cocktail enthusiasts consider the 2-in-1 zester and peeler a must-have because it makes it easy to separate the vibrant zest from the bitter pith.
- ✦ Channel Knife: This classic bar tool is essential if you're looking to create swanky garnishes.
- ✦ Pronged Tip Bar Knife: The long, thin handle makes elaborate cuts a cinch, while the tip makes it easy to add a cherry or olive to a drink.
- ✦ "Y" Garnish Peeler: A professional piece of kit for the urbane cocktail aficionado,

the *Y* stands for "yes" in terms of pulling off whatever it is charged with.

Since citrus can contribute much more than a lovely garnish to a cocktail, you'll also want to consider the following items if you're looking to extract everything you can from these zesty fruits.

✦ Rimmer with Citrus Well: A lovely addition that makes it easy to add salt or sugar to the rim of a glass, while the citrus well holds citrus wedges or strips of zest to add once the cocktail has been constructed.

✦ Citrus Juicer: It resembles an ice cream scoop, only with two scoops, one resting on top of the other. Place a citrus half in one and squeeze to get every last drop of juice, knowing that the built-in strainer will keep any seeds from making their way into your drink.

✦ Citrus Reamer: The classic, albeit medieval-looking reamer uses its tapered blade to capture all the tart and tangy pulp and juice.

HOW TO CRAFT CITRUS GARNISHES

Always wash and dry the fruit thoroughly before creating a garnish. While it's best to make citrus-based garnishes as close to cocktail hour as possible, they can be created well in advance—which is especially helpful when you're considering one of the more elaborate constructions.

Citrus can be kept at room temperature for several days and in the refrigerator for up to a week. Don't store citrus in a container, as this will only cause the citrus to become overly ripe.

If you find yourself with citrus that is about to spoil, you can cut it up and freeze the pieces.

Zest

It's just as fun to utter this pleasant word as it is to create. Practice until you know the right amount of pressure required to separate the colored portion of the peel from the white pith.

Using a citrus zester: Apply pressure and drag the sharp edge down the fruit. You will produce long, thin, curly strips of zest that can be used singularly or combined to produce tantalizing garnishes.

Using a microplane: Over a cutting board or plate, hold the microplane in one hand, apply moderate pressure, and drag the microplane downward, turning the fruit as you go to avoid removing the pith. The zest will gather in the groove on the underside of the microplane.

Using a vegetable peeler: Perfect for creating long, thick strips, work around the citrus to create pieces that are easy to twist.

Using a paring knife: Sharpen the knife, place it between the zest and pith and, while applying moderate pressure, twist the fruit to remove the required length.

Wedge: This ubiquitous garnish does require a bit of technique. First, slice a ¼" off each end of a citrus fruit. Next, cut the fruit in half, lengthwise, and set one of the halves cut side down on your cutting board. Finally, slice it at an angle, lengthwise, and you should have a perfect wedge. You want to aim for moderate-sized wedges that allow the drinker to readily squeeze the juice into their beverage. Slice a small cut in the midsection of the wedge so that it can sit on the rim of a glass. You can set out your garnished glasses

pre-party or place the wedges in glass bowls in order to show off their colorful skins.

Wheel: Cut a wheel by slicing the citrus fruit in half crosswise. Make another parallel cut about ⅛" to ¼" up from the initial cut. As a wheel rests on the rim of a glass, make another cut from the center of the wheel out to the edge.

Twist: Twists are used in a variety of drinks, especially those enduring, classic cocktails. Producing a twist requires a knife—ideally the

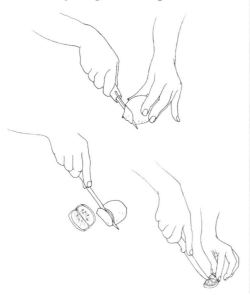

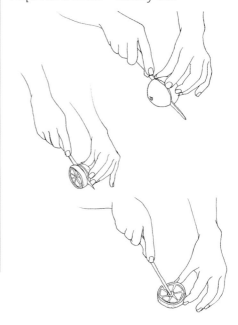

U-shaped blade of a channel knife. To create a daintier twist, hold the citrus fruit in one hand, the channel knife in the other, and cut a strip of zest about 3" long. The zest will emerge from the channel knife's center "window," so you can judge the length. Once you have the desired amount of zest, hold it over the surface of your cocktail, twist into a tight spiral, and release it into the drink, expressing the oils and adding a refreshing visual.

Tattoo: An easy-to-make garnish with unlimited options. Why? Scoring the citrus with a zester or serrated knife allows you to choose any design you want—from abstract shapes and easily recognizable logos to your own "cocktail crest." Simply hold the citrus at a slight angle in one hand, and, with the zester in your other hand, score the fruit from top to bottom; repeat around the citrus. Cut the fruit at the midsection, and fashion into wedges or wheels.

In addition, a tattooed citrus shell, with its designed side up, is a pretty holder for toothpicks, cocktail umbrellas, cocktail forks, and other accessories.

A tattooed citrus half is also the perfect foundation for a Flaming Citrus Shell—a dramatic garnish for tiki drinks. Use a citrus juicer to remove the juice and mold the shell back into shape, smoothing out any fruit fiber. This is your vessel. Place a sugar cube or crouton soaked in overproof rum or lemon extract in the center to serve as the wick. If you're looking to extend the show, use lemon extract, because it will remain alight a bit longer than the rum will. Float the citrus shell in the drink and light the cube. When the flame burns out—bottoms up!

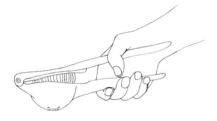

Scored Citrus: The scored citrus is a designed wheel that lends itself to the larger surface area provided by oranges, grapefruits, and tangelos. Using a channel knife or serrated knife, remove a strip of peel from the top of the fruit to the bottom. Repeat on the opposite side of the fruit. Repeat three or more times so you have equidistant lines on the fruit. Cut the citrus at the midsection to

fashion wheels or slices for garnishes that will be perfect in a Negroni or floating in a punch bowl.

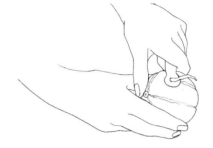

Citrus Knot: Cut strips of peel from the fruit with a vegetable peeler or a paring knife. Scrape off the white pith, cut the strips into 3"-by-$\frac{1}{2}$" pieces, and tie each piece into a knot.

Citrus Basket: Using key limes, makrut limes, or dwarf lemons to create handled citrus "baskets" that hold edible seeds (such as pomegranate, watermelon, persimmon, akebia, melon, etc.) is a stunning yet whimsical layered look. Cut the citrus while either holding it in one hand or placing it on a cutting board. Using a channel knife or serrated knife, cut a wide strip in

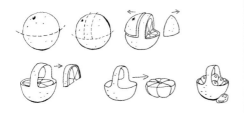

the vertical midsection of the fruit, working from the top to the equator. Cut around the strip and remove the two sections of fruit. Carefully cut the fruit away from the underside of the wide strip to make a "basket handle." Carefully remove the pulp from the bottom half of the fruit. Mold back into shape and fill the basket with a few of the edible seeds.

Sculpted Citrus Garnishes

Citrus peels readily lend themselves to being shaped. Irresistibly charming, these avatars require some work, but the look is the epitome of cocktail couture.

Flower: This is a "gateway garnish," as it is the simplest of the group to make. Using a vegetable peeler or a "Y" garnish peeler, hold the fruit in one hand or place it on a cutting board. Start at one end and cut a long, thin strip of peel. Starting at one end of the strip, wrap as tightly as possible to form a floret. You can secure with a small toothpick or, alternatively, allow the florets to open and "bloom.".

Butterfly: Using a vegetable peeler or a "Y" garnish peeler, cut a thin strip of peel from each side of the citrus fruit. Cut the strips into 1"-long pieces. Cut the fruit into thin wheels and then cut the wheels into thirds. To assemble the butterfly, place two thirds from a wheel on a clean citrus leaf with the pointed ends touching. Use two of the 1"-long strips as the antennae. Float the butterflies in a drink or a punch bowl.

Ship: Ahoy! Using a serrated knife, cut a lemon or lime into eight wedges. Take a wedge, cut straight across the top, and remove the center section. Cut a thin strip from the peel of a different citrus fruit (orange, tangerine, or pummelo, for example) to create the ship's "sail." Stand a toothpick in the center of the wedge. Skewer the strip of peel to create the sail. Cut a cherry into quarters and add one of the cherry pieces to the tip of the toothpick to make a flag! You can also use a cranberry or a blueberry as your flag.

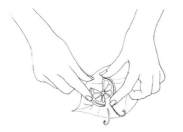

CITRUS CHAMPAGNE CELEBRATION

Drinking champagne and sparkling wine from the world's best vineyards is one of life's more pleasurable experiences; luxury and joy pour straight from the bottle. But decadent bubbly also plays nice with a variety of fruit juices and spirits, such as peach juice (for a much-loved Bellini), orange juice (for the ultimate brunch cocktail, the Mimosa), raspberry liqueur, Campari, cognac, brandy (especially cherry), and crème de cassis. Here champagne teams up with blood orange liqueur for a cocktail that is certain to dazzle your eyes—and taste buds.

1/4 oz. Solerno Blood Orange Liqueur

1/4 oz. Bacardi rum, Grey Goose vodka, or Absolut Citron vodka

1/2 oz. champagne

Place all of the ingredients in a cocktail shaker filled with ice and shake gently.

Strain into a champagne flute.

FINISHING TOUCHES
Use pinking shears to scallop the ends of a strip of lemon peel and drop it into the cocktail. A slice of blood orange perched on the flute's rim will call attention to the drink's vibrant nature.

TOURIST TRAP

This tiki-inspired cocktail is an expression of Jamaica's rich rum tradition. Mixed with flavors and spices native to the island, it is served in a vessel one might find in the eclectic shops along the shoreline of Negril's beautiful Seven Mile Beach.

**Josh Suchan, beverage director at Skylight Gardens
and founder of Ice and Alchemy, Los Angeles**

2 oz. rum blend

1 oz. fresh lime juice

1 oz. tiki mix

1/4 oz. Orgeat (see page 207)

2 dashes of Bittercube
Jamaican Bitters

Place the rum blend, lime juice, tiki mix, and Orgeat in the serving glass—a tiki mug or specialty glass—and then fill with crushed ice.

Use the swizzle method to combine the drink. Place a swizzle stick between your hands, lower the swizzle stick into the drink, and quickly rub your palms together to rotate the stick. Top with more crushed ice and the bitters.

FINISHING TOUCHES
Perch a bouquet of mint and a mango fan atop the crushed ice. To make the bouquet, remove the top portions from five sprigs of fresh, young mint and group them into a bouquet. To make the mango fan, cut three thin slices from mango. Pivot the slices at one end to form a fan and skewer that end with a bamboo cocktail pick.

For rum blend: Combine 1 cup Appleton Estate White rum, 1 cup Appleton Estate VX rum, 1/2 cup Smith & Cross rum, and 1/4 cup coconut oil and let sit for 3 days or until desired flavor is achieved. Place in the freezer until the oil hardens and accumulates on top of the liquid. Remove the hardened oil and transfer the rum blend into a bottle.

For tiki mix: Place 1 cup pineapple juice, 1/2 grated nutmeg seed, 1/2 oz. St. Elizabeth Allspice Dram, 1/4 oz. Angostura bitters, and 1 large cinnamon stick in a blender and puree for 30 seconds. Strain and store in the refrigerator.

HENNESSY WILDFLOWER

The use of wildflower honey matters here—using clove honey or lavender honey would keep this cocktail from its intended effect. The lemon-based garnishes reinforce the bright and tart notes in the drink, and allow the lighter aspects—specifically the floral tones of the honey—to make themselves known.

Jordan Bushell, national brand ambassador at Hennessy

2 oz. Hennessy V.S.O.P Privilège

1/2 oz. fresh lime juice

1/2 oz. fresh lemon juice

1 oz. honey syrup, made with wildflower honey

Place all of the ingredients in a cocktail shaker filled with ice and shake until chilled.

Strain into a stemless wine glass containing fresh ice.

FINISHING TOUCHES

Garnish with a dash of lemon zest and a lemon twist.

For honey syrup: Place equal parts honey and water in a saucepan and cook, while stirring, over medium heat until the honey has dissolved.

SIDECAR

The Ritz Hotel in Paris claims to be the birthplace of the Sidecar, the iconic cognac cocktail. But the sugared rim we associate with it today was added at the Savoy, the famous London hotel. The sugar rim adds a necessary bit of sweetness and also links the Sidecar to an even older cognac-based classic, the Brandy Crusta.

Jordan Bushell, national brand ambassador at Hennessy

sugar, for the rim

2 oz. Hennessy V.S or V.S.O.P

3/4 oz. Grand Marnier

1/2 oz. fresh lemon juice

Wet the rim of a chilled coupe or cocktail glass and dip it into the sugar.

Place the remaining ingredients in a cocktail shaker filled with ice and shake until chilled.

Strain into the rimmed glass.

FINISHING TOUCHES
Garnish with a twist of lemon.

BETWEEN THE SHEETS

Rum adds complexity to this twist on the Sidecar. Tart and refreshing, this cocktail is intriguing for its slightly risqué name and breathtaking simplicity.

Jordan Bushell, national brand ambassador at Hennessy

1 oz. Hennessy V.S.O.P Privilège

1 oz. 3- to 5-year-old rum

1 oz. Grand Marnier

½ oz. fresh lemon juice

Place all of the ingredients in a cocktail shaker filled with ice and shake until chilled.

Strain into a coupe or cocktail glass.

FINISHING TOUCHES
In keeping with the cocktail's celebration of simplicity, garnish with nothing more than a twist of lemon.

CUTTY CRUSTA

One of the earliest cocktails, the Crusta was served in a stemmed wine glass with a sugared rim, ushering in the concept of the "fancy cocktail." The Cutty Crusta utilizes Cutty Sark's Prohibition Scotch to update this classic.

Gareth Howells, bar manager and bartender at Forrest Point, Brooklyn

sugar, for the rim

1½ oz. Cutty Sark Prohibition Scotch

¾ oz. Cointreau

1 barspoon of maraschino liqueur

½ oz. fresh lemon juice

½ oz. simple syrup

2 dashes of Angostura bitters

Wet the rim of a chilled coupe and dip it into the sugar.

Place the remaining ingredients in a cocktail shaker filled with ice and shake vigorously until chilled.

Double-strain into the rimmed glass.

FINISHING TOUCHES
Wrap a lemon peel flower (see page 77) around a maraschino cherry, which will serve as the flower's center.

VIEUX CARRÉ

This drink shares its name with the famed French Quarter of New Orleans, and its spiritual home is the Carousel Bar in the Hotel Monteleone. When made right, the enticing balance of flavors will pull you in and never let you go. With cognac and rye whiskey sharing the spotlight, this cocktail is the epitome of the French-American fusion that makes New Orleans so unique. With a delicious, boozy cocktail such as this, it's important to choose your garnishes wisely, and a lemon twist and maraschino cherry provide the ideal accents.

Jordan Bushell, national brand ambassador for Hennessy

1 oz. Hennessy V.S.O.P Privilège
1 oz. rye whiskey
1 oz. sweet vermouth
splash of Bénédictine
dash of Angostura bitters
dash of Peychaud's bitters

Place all of the ingredients in a mixing glass filled with ice and stir until chilled.

Strain into an Old Fashioned glass.

FINISHING TOUCHES
Garnish with a twist of lemon and a maraschino cherry.

COMPADRE

This decadent drink originated in 1930s New Orleans and was then modified to soften the two base spirits with the sherry and Bénédictine. A cat that hangs around the Hennessy photo studio lent its name to this drink, but the appellation also fits the fast friendship between the cognac and rye.

Jordan Bushell, national brand ambassador for Hennessy

1 oz. Hennessy V.S
1 oz. Bulleit Rye whiskey
2 barspoons of oloroso sherry
1 barspoon of Bénédictine
dash of Angostura bitters

Place all of the ingredients in a mixing glass filled with ice and stir until chilled.

Strain into a coupe.

FINISHING TOUCHES
Garnish with an orange twist.

HIGHLANDER

Setting rum, Scotch, and amaro off with a bit of lemon oil and a slice of dehydrated orange will transport you to the beautiful, tucked-away beaches that Curaçao is famous for.

KJ Williams, bartender at Flatiron Lounge, New York

1¼ oz. tea-infused Scotch (Pig's Nose preferred)

1 oz. Hamilton 86 Demerara Rum

¾ oz. honey syrup (see page 85)

¾ oz. fresh lemon juice

¼ oz. Amaro CioCiaro

Place all of the ingredients in a cocktail shaker filled with ice and shake vigorously.

Strain over fresh ice into a double Old Fashioned glass.

FINISHING TOUCHES
Express a strip of lemon over the cocktail and drop it into the cocktail, then add a crescent-shaped slice of dehydrated orange.

For tea-infused Scotch: Place 2 bags of Lapsang souchong in 1 cup of Scotch and let stand overnight.

HERO WATER

"The Hero Water cocktail was made by accident, as most inventions are wont to do, in my kitchen while developing the menu for Ichicoro Ramen [in Tampa, FL]. There, all of the cocktails are made with a combination of both Japanese ingredients and those found locally in Florida—many times with a Latin influence," Wohlers says. "I love a good Piña Colada, but this time I wanted to try cucumber instead of pineapple, and it was a success. It is now Ichicoro Ramen's signature cocktail!"

Jessica Wohlers, general manager and mixologist at Leyenda, Brooklyn

---

2 oz. shochu

1 oz. fresh cucumber juice

3/4 oz. fresh lime juice

3/4 oz. Coco López Cream of Coconut

2 dashes of Angostura bitters

Place all of the ingredients in a cocktail shaker and shake vigorously.

Strain over ice into a double Old Fashioned glass.

FINISHING TOUCHES

Garnish with a lime wheel, a thin ribbon of cucumber, and a cocktail umbrella.

DUCHESS MARTINI

Anyone who knows me also knows that my signature drink is a pure, elegant, straight-up Martini—a preference I apparently share with Humphrey Bogart, FDR, Clark Gable, and, of course, James Bond. I drink a vodka Martini, and the vodka needs to come from potatoes—perhaps it's my Czech heritage, or my respect for the LiV vodka put out by Long Island Spirits. The distillery has been around since the 1800s, and their vodka is an example of what is available in most every region: a tasty sense of place, with distillation articulating the unique terroir.

3/4 to 1 oz. chilled potato vodka

1/2 oz. Dolin Blanc vermouth

Place the vodka and vermouth in a cocktail shaker filled with ice and shake vigorously.

Strain into a chilled cocktail glass.

For those who refuse to shake a Martini: Pour the vermouth into the chilled cocktail glass, swirl the glass to coat the sides, and then add the vodka.

FINISHING TOUCHES
Drop a long twist of lemon peel into the cocktail.

GARNISH BACKSTORY:
OLIVES

The olive has long been the rock star of garnishes. Not unlike other classic garnishes, the olive was first used because of its myriad health benefits. Martini olives are preserved in brine and add a salty taste to a cocktail. The use of brine-soaked olives in drinks was reportedly pioneered by a Syrian physician, Dr. Ammar Martini. Cocktail legend has it that after the French left Syria, Martini went to Paris and managed a bar and café, where he put an olive in each cocktail because Idlib province, where he was from, was known for its nourishing olives. He was a doctor, after all.

Most often, three green olives are used to garnish a Martini. It's a kind of tradition that following the first sip, one olive is consumed. The last olive or two accompany the last sip. Olive garnishes can also be stuffed with almonds, blue cheese, jalapeño peppers, or anchovies.

FLIRTY FRUITS

otanically speaking, fruits are the seed-bearing part of a flowering plant. The cornucopia of fruits that posh-up the flavor and appearance of cocktails includes bananas, pineapples, dragon fruits, blueberries, currants, cherry tomatoes, figs, grapes, pears, raspberries, strawberries, watermelons, pomegranates, peaches, blackberries, plums, avacadoes, peppers, and quinces.

Since brandy is distilled from fruit (mainly grapes, but also cherries, peaches, apples, and more than an orchard or two of other fruits), it's only natural that brandy-based drinks go well with a fruity garnish.

Distilling fruit to produce spirits such as brandy, pisco, and grappa has been a staple in almost every county around the world for centuries, and fruit-forward cognac is made by

aging the *eau-de-vie* (water of life) produced by the double distillation of white wine—in Cognac, France, of course.

You can also ferment fruit at home to create your own liquors or use fresh fruit to infuse spirits like vodka or gin.

Everyone knows how hard the beloved Old Fashioned cocktail leans on its orange-and-cherry garnish. One of the earliest cocktails, the Cobbler, also relied upon fruit's

sweetness to charm consumers more than 200 years ago. The basic recipe for a Cobbler consists of shaved or crushed ice—an exotic treat at the time—a spirit or wine, a bit of sugar, a slice of pineapple or orange, a pile of berries, and, when on hand, mint.

Shrubs hearken to the Colonial era, when using vinegar to preserve fruits was essential. Before long, shrubs and spirits were combined to make drinks that balanced sweet and sour. Recently, shrubs have returned to prominence, popping up everywhere from cocktail culture hot spots to at-home happy hours.

The classic shrub is extremely simple to prepare: just heat up equal parts sugar and vinegar until the former dissolves, pour the mixture over some cut-up fruit, and let stand for a while. A popular recipe features 2 cups sugar, 2 cups vinegar, and 1 pound fruit.

Using vinegar to pickle a fruit is another way to hold onto the flavor of a particular season. Strawberries, apples, and stone fruits are especially good pickled.

Fruit garnishes are the two-to-tango complement to a countless number of cocktails, with their beauty and refreshing, delicious flavors providing an inimitable kind of ballast.

Moreover, fruit garnishes can be presented in a number of distinctive forms: freshly sliced, dehydrated, chopped, frozen, sugar-coated, and combined with other fruits, herbs, or flowers. Certain fruits—such as apples, strawberries, pineapples, and pretty-in-pink, polka-dotted dragon fruits—can be shaped into fanciful, dreamy designs.

Apples, sliced and skewered on a cocktail pick, make for a vibrant garnish in all of their shades—just be sure to rub the inside with lemon so that the flesh doesn't brown— and are especially toothsome when paired with an apple brandy–based cocktail, such as the I Cannot Tell a Lie (see page 114).

Cocktail culture's classic *Trader*

Vic's Bartender's Guide embraced fruit garnishes and set the stage for you to make a Carmen Miranda-esque statement with your ornamentation of tropical cocktails, which scream out for fruits to mingle with the rum, citrus, and orgeat.

Lest you forget: coffee is a stone fruit, just like a cherry, and both can add drama to a number of drinks. Three coffee beans—representing health, happiness, and prosperity—have long been recognized as the standard garnish for a glass of Sambuca. Today, that trio has migrated to other cocktails, notably the Espresso Martini, where the three coffee beans can be arranged to reflect a flower petal afloat on the drink's foamy top.

MARASCHINO CHERRIES

A staple of cocktail garnishes, the history of the maraschino cherry is wrapped up in world politics and geography. A favorite of

European aristocracy, the authentic maraschino—the marasca cherry—is grown only in the sandy soils of Croatia's Dalmatian mountains. Those whole cherries, which were preserved in liqueur, became forbidden in the United States during Prohibition, allowing the bright red impostor most associated with the term *maraschino* to arise.

Luxardo, founded in 1821 on the Croatian coast, is the original maraschino cherry distillery. The elegant liqueur was quickly embraced by fine establishments in the United States, only to be similarly pushed aside by Prohibition. However, its popularity has started to rebound, with its slightly nutty and sour (that's right, it's not sweet) flavor popping up in a number of innovative cocktails.

If you're looking for a garnish that can play off the sweet vermouth in a bespoke Manhattan or take the bite out of a bourbon-based cocktail, bypass the syrupy charlatan and turn to the real thing.

SELECTING FRUIT

When selecting fresh fruit for garnish, peruse the farmers markets or fresh produce sections of supermarkets and international markets. No Chinatown or Little Havana in your area? Order online from a burgeoning web-based global market—especially for fruits from faraway lands. Or grow your own. I grow citrus and berries indoors all year long, and the aesthetics, ease, and taste can't be beat.

While no fruit will ever look as perfect as it does in an ad, it should not have black or brown spots or holes in the skin. Smell the fruit for freshness and squeeze it to insure firmness.

Always wash all fruit in cold water, and pat dry with a towel. If the fruit is not organic, it is recommended that you soak it in salty water or baking soda before washing to remove the chemicals used on factory farms.

Frozen fruit and quality canned fruit are some other tasty options to utilize fruit in your cocktails. When I make maraschino cherries, I often used canned cherries from Michigan or Oregon if fresh cherries are out of season; I do the same with peaches if I simply must have a Bellini in February.

And don't overlook dehydrated fruits, which can be used to create terrific garnishes and are readily available.

It should go without saying that citrus and other fruits go together like sun and sand, so feel free to mix and match garnishes. I personally love wrapping citrus peels around strawberries and cherries and securing them with ornamental pins.

THE ART OF FRUIT GARNISH

Fan Garnish: Strawberries and apples are especially good for fan garnishes. Place the washed and dried fruit on a cutting board. Using a paring knife, make several thin slices in the fruit (or piece of fruit) without cutting through the top, leaving the slices attached to the hull or skin. Pull apart the slices so that they fan out, while making sure they remain attached to the hull or skin. Float on top of the drink or rest on the side of the glass, with one or two of the fans inside the glass and one on the outside.

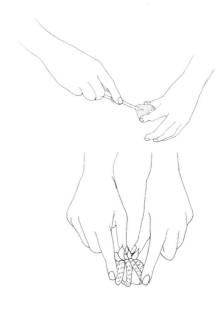

Cherry, Currant, or Cranberry Flowers: Place the fresh, whole fruit on a cutting board. Cut the top third of the fruit into four to six wedges with a sharp paring knife. Use the tip of the knife to gently separate the remaining segments until the fruit resembles a flower petal. Feel free to add another fruit, a piece of candied ginger, chocolate, or mint leaves for added decoration.

Pineapples

Fresh, sweet pineapples can be sliced or quartered with a knife. Cut into wheels and make a slit in the center of each wheel so that they can perch on a glass's rim. Or cut into chunks, place on a skewer with cherries, and float in the drink.

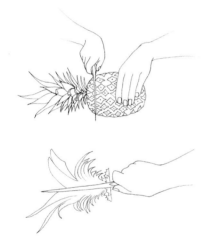

An exotic tiki garnish is the Pineapple Firebird. The leaves at the top are the bird's "tail." To create, you'll need a knife, a maraschino cherry with its stem, and a toothpick.

Remove the top of the pineapple about an inch from the base of the leaves. Vertically section the pineapple top into 4 to 6 sections (depending on size of fruit) so that each section has a bit of pineapple flesh and a plume of leaves. Cut a slit at a 45-degree angle from the inner flesh toward the pineapple shell. Insert the toothpick vertically through the smaller segment of flesh. Put a cherry on the toothpick and position the garnish so that the stem hangs over the beverage, giving the illusion that the "bird" is drinking from the glass.

You can also use a pineapple as a drinking vessel. Just slice off the top and carve a space for a straw in it. Hollow out the inside of the pineapple, and freeze both pieces until cocktail hour. Fill the shell with your cocktail, add the leafy top, insert straw, and soak in the tropical vibes.

Pickled Strawberries, Apples, and Stone Fruits

Mix 2 to 3 pounds of fruit with 2 cups of sugar and ¼ teaspoon salt until the fruit is coated and let stand at room temperature for 10 to 12 hours.

Strain, reserve the fruit, and transfer the liquid to a medium saucepan with 3/4 cup red wine vinegar and 1/2 cup simple syrup. Cook over high heat until the mixture is syrupy, about 5 minutes, then pour over the fruit and let stand for another 12 hours. Repeat this step every 12 hours or so until the desired flavor is achieved. Once you are satisfied with the flavor of the syrup, let it cool completely.

Pour the cooled liquid over the fruit, pressing down on the fruit until it's covered. Transfer to clean, sanitized mason jars and store for up to 1 month in the refrigerator, or can and store for up to 1 year.

For quicker pickled fruit, cover with brine that is 3 parts water to 1 part vinegar and let stand for 1 hour.

As pickled fruit is tangy, tart, and sweet, think about pairing it with a vanilla syrup to provide flavor balance.

Cherry blossoms are wonderful pickled. Gather 2 cups of cherry blossoms just before they are in full bloom, rinse, sprinkle with salt, and massage it into the blossoms. Cover with water and soak for 3 days. After 3 days, strain and squeeze the blossoms to remove all of the liquid. Reserve the liquid for another preparation. Transfer the blossoms to a mason jar, cover with plum vinegar, and refrigerate for 2 to 3 days. Drain and dry the blossoms. They will have a tart flavor with hints of cherry and almond.

To use pickled fruit as a cocktail garnish, simply float it in a drink or skewer several pieces and balance on the glass's rim. You can also wrap the pickled fruit in edible leaves, such as the moringa (the "tree of life," touted as a superfood), mulberry, or hibiscus.

Berry Spears, Cozies, and Mushrooms

Skewer one or more seasonal berries and place the pick across the top of the glass for a "berry" dramatic garnish. If you're focused on keeping your guests cool and refreshed, freeze the skewers before dropping them into the drinks.

Create Berry Cozies by stuffing a raspberry with a blueberry, using fresh or frozen fruit. To add another level of fun to this floral-looking garnish, use icing or chocolate shavings to make a design on the blueberry.

Remove the top of an apple with a corer and place a raspberry on the top to echo the look of a mushroom. Float these in a cocktail or punch bowl, or use a toothpick to fasten them to slices of kiwi before setting them adrift.

Banana Dolphin

Brian Miller, of Death & Co., Tiki Mondays with Miller, and Mother's Ruin fame and now partner, beverage director, and bartender at The Polynesian—New York's first tiki joint since Trader Vic's—details his method for this dramatic tour de force:

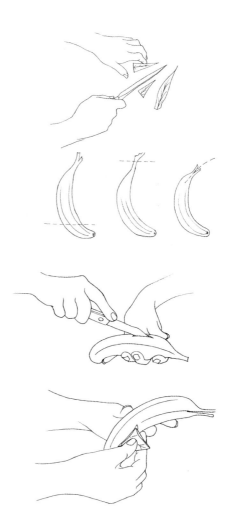

"Shape three 'fins' for the tiki dolphin out of pineapple leaves. Remove any brown areas from the leaves and make sure your leaf selections are green and firm. Two of the leaves should be the same size (these will be the flippers), and the third leaf should be bigger and will become the fin.

"Cut off the bottom fifth of banana. Slice off a quarter inch of the stem tip of the banana. Slice through the stem to make the dolphin's mouth. Make a slit at the top part of the banana (the dolphin's back) and insert the larger of the pineapple leaves.

"Make two slits at the sides of the peel about halfway down the banana. Insert the smaller pineapple leaves to create the flippers. Next, make a slit at a 45-degree angle about an inch from the bottom of the banana. This is how you will make the dolphin stand on the lip of the glass."

HOMEMADE MARASCHINO CHERRIES

These will take you beyond the cloyingly sweet impostor clogging the shelves at your local grocery store, highlighting the slightly sour flavor of the cherry.

peel of 1 orange

1 cup water

1 cup sugar

seeds from 1/2 vanilla pod

2 teaspoons fresh lemon juice

1 cinnamon stick

pinch of nutmeg

1 lb. in-season cherries, pitted (or canned sweet cherries from Oregon or Michigan)

1 cup cherry liqueur (optional)

Place all of the ingredients, except for the cherries and the liqueur, in a saucepan and bring to a boil over medium-high heat. Reduce heat so that the mixture simmers.

Add the cherries and simmer for 5 minutes (less time is needed if using canned cherries).

Remove the saucepan from heat and add the cherry liqueur. Let cool and store in an airtight container.

I CANNOT TELL A LIE

Since 1698, the Laird family has produced applejack in New Jersey. Laird & Company is America's first distillery, and their products were so beloved during the Colonial era that George Washington once wrote to the family requesting their applejack recipe. Washington's diary entries from the following years contain a number of references to his personal production of "cyder spirits."

½ oz. Laird's Applejack

¼ oz. caramel syrup

1 oz. apple sparkling water

4 dashes of Fee Brothers Aztec Chocolate Bitters

Place all of the ingredients in a cocktail shaker filled with ice and shake vigorously.

Strain over ice into a highball glass.

FINISHING TOUCHES
Rest an apple fan (see page 107) on the glass's rim and add a cinnamon stick. Be sure to brush the apple's flesh with lemon juice to prevent browning.

For caramel syrup: Place 1 oz. of caramel extract, 1 cup of water, and 1 cup of sugar in a saucepan and cook, while stirring, over medium heat until the sugar has dissolved. Remove from heat, let cool, and store in the refrigerator for up to 1 month.

SUPERSTORM

They were making Hurricanes fast and furiously at Fitzgerald's the night Hurricane Sandy hit New York. The event precipitated Tom and his fellow bartenders' discovery that the bar guide had changed the recipe—a modification they didn't like. The Hurricane had become one of the bar's signature drinks, so when Sandy was "downgraded" to a superstorm, they decided that the original Hurricane also needed to be reclassified. As you'll soon see for yourself, this version's a definite upgrade.

Tom Sebazco, entrepreneur and bartender at Fitzgerald's Pub, New York

1¼ oz. spiced rum
1 oz. Midori
1 oz. amaretto
2 oz. pineapple juice
2 oz. orange juice
dash of grenadine
splash of soda water

Place all of the ingredients, except for the soda water, in a mixing glass filled with ice and stir.

Pour the contents into a pint glass and top with the soda water.

FINISHING TOUCHES
Garnish with pineapple and orange wedges and either a fresh, in-season cherry or a Homemade Maraschino Cherry (see page 113).

APPLE SHRUB COCKTAIL

A shrub is a style of drink that was used to preserve fruit before refrigeration. This cocktail is sure to warm you in the depths of winter, but it can be turned to any time you're in the mood for a complex, bold drink. The tart, sour notes of apple cider vinegar in the gastrique are a natural balance to an apple's natural sweetness. The quintessentially American flavors of apple and cinnamon in the garnish pair perfectly with the drink's two main flavors, clueing the recipient in to what they can expect upon venturing further.

Jordan Bushell, national brand ambassador for Hennessy

---

1 oz. apple cider gastrique

1¹/₂ oz. Hennessy V.S

¹/₂ oz. zubrówka (bison grass vodka)

2 dashes of Angostura bitters

Place all of the ingredients in a mixing glass filled with ice and stir until chilled.

Strain into an Old Fashioned glass containing a large ice cube.

FINISHING TOUCHES
Garnish with an apple fan (see page 107) and freshly grated cinnamon.

For apple cider gastrique: Place 1¹/₃ cups brown sugar and 1¹/₃ cups water in a saucepan and bring to a boil. Add 2 cups of diced Royal Gala apples, reduce the heat, and simmer for 30 minutes. Add 1 cup apple cider vinegar, raise the heat, and return to a boil. Reduce the heat and simmer for 30 minutes. Remove from heat, let cool, and then strain through cheesecloth.

CANTALOUPE FRESCA

Fresca is Spanish for "fresh," and pitting bright elderflower and robust Hennessy against the light, sweet nature of cantaloupe makes for a uniquely refreshing experience.

Jordan Bushell, national brand ambassador for Hennessy

½ oz. cantaloupe agua fresca

1½ oz. Hennessy V.S

½ oz. St-Germain

Place the ingredients in a Collins glass filled with ice and stir until chilled.

FINISHING TOUCHES

Garnish with a chunk or ball of cantaloupe.

For cantaloupe agua fresca: Place 4 cups water, 4 cups chopped cantaloupe, 2 tablespoons white sugar, and 1 oz. fresh lime juice in a container, stir until the sugar is dissolved, and let sit for at least 6 hours. Chill in the refrigerator before serving.

AMY'S AMOUR

Amy, my cousin, is a true Jersey girl. This drink is a tribute to her husband Jeff and their marriage. An Old Fashioned gets some Garden State love by adding a bit of Laird's Applejack, making for a smoky love potion, er, cocktail.

1/2 oz. high-quality bourbon

1/4 oz. Laird's Applejack

1/2 oz. black tea, chilled

1/3 oz. Lapsang souchong & vanilla syrup

3 to 4 dashes of Fee Brothers Cherry Bitters

Add the ingredients to a mixing glass filled with ice in the order that they are listed and stir.

Strain over ice into an Old Fashioned glass.

FINISHING TOUCHES
Garnish with Homemade Maraschino Cherries (see page 113) or Luxardo maraschino cherries, a splash of the liquid from the cherries, and the scraped vanilla bean pod from the syrup.

For Lapsang souchong & vanilla syrup: Place 1 cup of water and 1 cup of sugar in a saucepan and cook, while stirring, over medium heat until the sugar is dissolved. Remove from heat, add 2 to 3 teaspoons of Lapsang souchong tea (depending on the desired level of smokiness) and the seeds from half of a vanilla bean pod. Let stand until cool, strain, and store in the refrigerator.

FALLEN ANGEL

This twist on the Missionary's Downfall was inspired by the Billy Joel song "Only the Good Die Young."

Brian Miller, partner, bartender, and beverage director at The Polynesian, New York

3 sprigs of mint

dash of orange blossom honey

1/2 oz. fresh lime juice

1 oz. pineapple juice

1/2 oz. rich honey syrup (see page 85; use 2:1 honey-to-water ratio)

1/2 oz. Giffard Banane du Brésil

1 1/2 oz. Ron Zacapa rum

Place the mint in a cocktail shaker and gently muddle. Add the remaining ingredients and 3 ice cubes and shake until chilled.

Strain over crushed ice into a tiki mug or wine glass.

FINISHING TOUCHES
Garnish with additional sprigs of mint and a Banana Dolphin (see pages 110–11).

COGNAC KING KONG

A take on the classic King Kong, the king of tiki cocktails, this drink is more than strong enough to scale skyscrapers. You wouldn't think it, but cognac and rum bring similar elements to the table: a deep flavor that results from barrel aging, sweetness, and an agreeable nature that begs to be mixed. Tiki cocktails are great for letting your garnish imagination run wild, opening the door for daring visuals and tastes.

Jordan Bushell, national brand ambassador for Hennessy

1½ oz. Hennessy V.S

½ oz. Giffard Banane du Brésil

½ oz. falernum or spiced syrup

1 oz. fresh lemon juice

3 oz. pineapple juice

Place the ingredients in a cocktail shaker filled with ice and shake vigorously.

Strain over crushed ice into a tiki mug or highball glass.

FINISHING TOUCHES
Top with a dash of grenadine and freshly grated cinnamon, then carefully arrange a pineapple chunk and Banana Dolphin (see pages 110–11) on the glass.

BLACKBERRY DERBY

The Mint Julep is a classic that epitomizes the turn toward summer, a shift that is always signaled by the swarms of elaborate hats and sterling cups that descend on the Kentucky Derby each May. Josh wanted to expand upon that feeling, using sunflower seeds to accentuate the flavors of bourbon and a blackberry-honey gastrique to celebrate one of summer's greatest gifts.

**Josh Suchan, beverage director at Skylight Gardens
and founder of Ice and Alchemy, Los Angeles**

8 to 10 mint leaves

1/2 oz. blackberry-honey gastrique

2 oz. sunflower seed–infused bourbon

2 dashes of Angostura bitters

Place the mint leaves and blackberry-honey gastrique in a Julep cup and muddle.

Add the bourbon and add crushed ice until the cup is nearly full.

Mix the ingredients with a spoon until the tin is nicely frosted.

Top with a mound of crushed ice and the bitters.

FINISHING TOUCHES
Garnish with a bouquet of mint and skewered fresh blackberries.

For sunflower seed–infused bourbon: Combine 4 cups bourbon and 1/2 cup salted sunflower seeds in a container and let stand for 8 hours, or until desired flavor is achieved. Strain into a bottle.

For blackberry-honey gastrique: Place 1 cup clover honey in a saucepan and warm over medium heat for approximately 5 minutes. Add 1 cup of Lucero Blackberry Red Balsamic Vinegar, stir constantly for 1 minute, and then remove the saucepan from heat. Add 1 cup of room-temperature water and let the gastrique cool completely before bottling. Store in the refrigerator.

COLCA SOUR

Colca Canyon is outside of Arequipa, the second-largest city in Peru. The canyon is famous for its condors and natural preserve, but it also boasts a very peculiar fruit called the sancayo, *which grows on a cactus of the same name. The* sancayo *fruit is sour and bitter and looks like a green dragon fruit—which is what you'll want to use if you can't get your hands on any* sancayo.

Isaac Morrison, drink consultant at Dash Concept

½ oz. honey syrup (see page 85)

¾ oz. fresh *sancayo* juice

½ oz. Lillet Blanc

1½ oz. Macchu Pisco

dash of Amargo Chuncho bitters

1 egg white

Place the ingredients in a cocktail shaker filled with ice and give it a hard, quick shake.

Double-strain into a champagne or sommelier flute.

FINISHING TOUCHES
Delicately place ½ teaspoon of *sancayo* seeds on the foam. If locating the *sancayo* at the market is too challenging, you can use kiwi or green dragon fruit seeds as a substitute. To get enough seeds, scrape them into a fine sieve and rinse under water to remove the pulp.

HOLY WATER

This cocktail stems from Fabiano's frustration with the pettiness at the center of the argument that has been raging between Chileans and Peruvians for years: who invented pisco? The Spanish conquistadors, who brought the grapes that are the basis of the spirit, conquered the Incan Empire and established the Viceroyalty of Peru in the sixteenth century. It was in this administrative district, which predates the formation of both nations, that pisco was born. "Everyone needs to chill out and work together—just like in this drink!" Featuring a pisco from each country, everyone who encounters this lovely beverage will walk away feeling blessed.

Fabiano Latham, beverage director for Chotto Matte, London

1 oz. Macchu La Diablada Pisco
2/3 oz. Kappa Pisco
1 oz. citric acid solution
2/3 oz. simple syrup

Approximately 1 hour before preparing the drink, place the bottles of pisco and the mixing glass in the freezer—they need to be as cold as possible to get the intended effect.

Place all of the ingredients and ice in the mixing glass and stir for 30 seconds. Strain into an Old Fashioned glass containing a block of crystal-clear ice.

FINISHING TOUCHES
Wipe the rim of the glass with a strip of lime zest.

For citric acid solution: Dissolve 1/2 oz. of citric acid in 2 cups of water.

ICE BLOCK NERDISTRY

Going with water straight from the tap when making ice cubes will result in cloudy cubes that could potentially wash away the other efforts you've made. For crystal-clear ice, you'll want to use distilled water. Boil the water twice and let cool completely before adding to the ice-cube trays.

You likely have also seen large cubes and intriguing spheres of ice in cocktails at your local hotspots. These are hand-carved by truly artisanal purveyors, but you can procure molds for home use if your knife skills aren't quite up to snuff.

MARIA'S MEAD: NECTAR OF THE GODDESSES

This heavenly sweet cocktail is inspired by mead, the world's oldest spirit. This sweet nectar—which is thought to be the mythical ambrosia of the Greek gods—was believed to be descended from the heavens.

¼ oz. Long Island Spirits LiV vodka (or preferred premium vodka)

¼ oz. Long Island Spirits Strawberry Sorbetta

½ oz. Owl's Brew White & Vine tea

¼ oz. fresh lemon juice

¼ oz. local honey

Place all of the ingredients in a cocktail shaker filled with ice and shake vigorously.

Strain into a white wine glass.

FINISHING TOUCHES
Garnish with a pickled or fresh strawberry that has been wrapped in a lemon twist and secured by an ornamental cocktail pick.

TULLAMORE D.E.W. ELEVENSES

The cocktail is named after a traditional late-morning break and centers around the unexpectedly marvelous pairing of Irish breakfast tea and whiskey.

Jane Maher, brand ambassador for Tullamore D.E.W.

1¹/₂ oz. Tullamore D.E.W.

2 barspoons of raspberry preserves

¹/₂ oz. lemon juice

1¹/₄ oz. Irish breakfast tea, at room temperature

Place all of the ingredients in a cocktail shaker filled with ice and shake vigorously.

Strain into a Collins glass filled with ice.

FINISHING TOUCHES
Garnish with a twist of lemon.

VIVA SANTANA

This is a tiki-style cocktail in that it's a tall drink served on crushed ice with tropical notes. Here, the lime-wheel garnish is purely ornamental. It catches your eye and provides a little color in an otherwise monochromatic drink. A dehydrated passion fruit slice used as a garnish takes the effect up a few notches. The passion fruit's striking green-rimmed, slightly pink center will capture every drinker's imagination and curiosity.

KJ Williams, bartender at Flatiron Lounge, New York

---

1 3/4 oz. Del Maguey VIDA mezcal

3/4 oz. fresh lime juice

1/2 oz. Orgeat (see page 207)

1/2 oz. Velvet Falernum

1/4 oz. passion fruit syrup (1:1 ratio of passion fruit puree to simple syrup)

Fill a tall highball or Collins glass with pellet or crushed ice and add all of the ingredients.

Use the swizzle method to combine (see page 82). When combined, add more ice, forming a kind of snow cone at the top of the glass.

FINISHING TOUCHES
Garnish with a slice of dehydrated passion fruit and a lime wheel.

WELCOME POMEGRANATE MARGARITA

Steeped in romance, art, and history, the pomegranate fruit was carried by desert caravans for its thirst-quenching juice. Here, its refreshing qualities and racy red color fashion a cocktail that is naturally sweet, aromatic, and pretty.

Daniel Aceves, mixologist at Azul Bar at the Hilton Los Cabos Beach & Golf Resort, Cabo San Lucas

1 lime wedge, for the rim

Tajín seasoning, for the rim

1 teaspoon tequila

1 oz. La Pinta pomegranate & tequila liqueur

1/2 oz. fresh lemon juice

1/2 oz. simple syrup

Rub rim of a chilled glass with the lime wedge and then dip it into the Tajín seasoning.

Combine the tequila, La Pinta, lemon juice, and simple syrup in a cocktail shaker filled with ice and shake vigorously.

Add a few ice cubes to the glass and then strain the contents of the cocktail shaker into it.

FINISHING TOUCHES
Perch a slice of fresh lime on the rim of the glass.

JUNGLE BABBLER

The Jungle Babbler is Ryan's riff on the Jungle Bird, a stone-cold tiki classic. While it's got a lot to say, all of it is worth lending an ear to.

Ryan Liloia, bartender at Clover Club and Leyenda, Brooklyn

½ barspoon demerara syrup

½ oz. tonga mix

½ oz. fresh lime juice

¾ oz. pineapple juice

¼ oz. Hamilton 151 Overproof Demerara Rum

½ oz. Pierre Ferrand cognac

¾ oz. Appleton Estate Reserve rum

¾ oz. El Dorado 3-Year-Old white rum

¼ oz. Campari

4 dashes of blackstrap rum

dash of absinthe

Place all of the ingredients in a cocktail shaker filled with ice and shake vigorously.

Strain into a Collins glass filled with crushed ice.

FINISHING TOUCHES

Cut an 1-inch long slit in the top of a pineapple wedge and insert 2 pineapple leaves. Place the garnish on the rim of the cocktail.

For demerara syrup: Substitute demerara sugar for granulated sugar in a standard simple syrup.

For tonga mix: Combine 1 cup pomegranate juice with no sugar added, 1 cup sugar, a dash of fresh lemon juice, and 2 to 3 drops of orange blossom water in a saucepan and warm, while stirring, over medium-low heat until the sugar is dissolved, taking care not to let the mixture come to a boil. Remove from heat and let cool completely. The resulting syrup is homemade grenadine, which can be stored on its own in the refrigerator for up to 1 month. To make the tonga mix, combine ½ cup of the homemade grenadine with 1 oz. passion fruit syrup (see page 139).

ISLAND TIME

The Island Time is garnished with the Cobra's Head to honor the drink that served as its inspiration: the Cobra's Fang, which, according to Ryan, "is the cocktail that got me really into tiki."

Ryan Liloia, bartender at Clover Club and Leyenda, Brooklyn

½ oz. fresh lemon juice

¼ oz. passion fruit syrup

½ oz. Orgeat (see page 207)

½ oz. falernum

½ oz. Lemon Hart 151 Overproof Demerara Rum

1 oz. El Dorado 3-Year-Old white rum

1 oz. Appleton Estate Reserve rum

dash of Angostura bitters

2 dashes of absinthe

Place all of the ingredients in a cocktail shaker filled with ice and shake vigorously.

Strain into an Old Fashioned glass filled with crushed ice.

FINISHING TOUCHES

COBRA'S HEAD GARNISH

To form the garnish, run a channel knife along the perimeter of a lime until you have a 4" strip of peel. Cut a separate lime into wedges. Remove the pulp from one of the wedges. This wedge will be used to form the head of the snake. Fold the snake's head in half and make two small holes in the top. Insert a whole clove into each hole, forming eyes. Use an orchid petal (or whatever food-grade flower petals you have on hand) to make the tongue. Fasten the head to the 4" strip of peel with a cocktail pick and place the garnish on the rim of the glass.

GARDEN TO
GLASS

Gardens are both beautiful and empowering. Look no further than the massive surge the farm-to-table movement has made since the turn of the twenty-first century. That same verve has also managed to revolutionize spirit and cocktail culture.

FLOWERS

Flower petals, blossoms, and blooms are the crown jewels in a garden of cocktail creations. Flowers inspire artists working in every medium, and mixologists are no exception. Offering fragrance, color, texture, beauty, flavor, no small number of health benefits, and overwhelming variety, the gifts flowers have the potential to bestow are never-ending. You can work off the color of a cocktail, the season, the theme

of a party, and, of course, the other ingredients when considering your finishing floral flourish.

Flower power was never more apparent than at the 2015 premiere for the James Bond film *Spectre*,

where guests were treated to 007's favorite cocktail, garnished with edible blossoms.

VEGETABLES

The celery stalk has become such an integral part of the Bloody Mary that, at this point, it would be fair to call them a married couple. You wouldn't think it, but this ubiquitous green stalk has a long history as a curative, with its medicinal use noted as far back as Homer's *Odyssey*. Knowing that it was long used to treat colds, the flu, digestive ailments, and issues with water retention, it makes sense that someone looking to take the edge off their hangover with a Bloody Mary would add a celery stalk as an additional restorative. But this happy union appears to have occurred entirely by accident. Legend has it that during the early 1960s, a customer at Chicago's famed Pump Room (which unfortunately closed in 2017) couldn't wait for his server to bring him a swizzle stick for his Bloody Mary. Taking matters into his own hands, he snatched a celery stalk from a nearby tray and was smitten by the element it added to the drink. Just like that, the celery stalk garnish became essential, clearing the palate and providing much-needed hydration after a night of drinking.

Other vegetables that work wonderfully as garnishes are asparagus, peppers—from jalapeños to pepperoncini—artichoke hearts, pea shoots and pods, onions, potatoes (as French fries or tater tots), cucumbers, and carrots.

And though it is not technically a vegetable, mushroom garnishes are rising in popularity. It seems there are as many mushrooms as stars in the sky, offering a spectrum of colors—from a blue oyster or a white button to the bright salmon hue of a brain mushroom—that should set a garnish savant's imagination ablaze.

Offering structure, style, and taste to a savory cocktail, it's well worth foraging—either in the woods or at your farmers market—for some fungi.

COCKTAIL ONIONS

Traditional cocktail onions are simply pearl onions (a relative of the leek), or silverskin onions that have been pickled in a brine featuring small amounts of turmeric and paprika so that they remain crunchy. Some claim that the cocktail onion provides the pleasant, savory, umami flavor that gourmands are constantly on the lookout for.

The curious thing about the cocktail onion is that, though well known and in possession of a long, colorful backstory featuring many individuals laying claim to its invention, it is codified in only one drink: the Gibson.

The oldest published recipe for the Gibson (the savory cousin to the Martini) is found in the 1908 book *The World's Drinks and How to Mix Them* by William Boothby.

Those claiming to have invented the Gibson and its close companion, the cocktail-onion garnish, include famed graphic artist Charles Dana Gibson, who is said to have requested the combo from the bartender at The Players. It's most likely Gibson was just trying to be different—he was an artist, after all—but it's also said that he was looking to "improve" upon the Martini (even though that's not possible). The stockbroker Walter Campbell Gibson claims that he invented the drink at the Ritz Hotel in Paris. A Hugh Simons Gibson claims he invented it while drinking with his chums at the Metropolitan Club. Finally, a skinny-dipping Walter D. K. Gibson claimed he created the Gibson at San Francisco's private Bohemian Club because "eating onions would prevent colds," an important concern considering

San Francisco's chilly summers. Whatever the story, the regal-looking Gibson has long been an object of affection, with scores of prominent citizens identifying the Gibson and its onion garnish as their cocktail of choice. Ernest Hemingway, the father of so much drinking lore, was said to garnish his Gibsons with plain frozen onions, which also helped keep his drink cold.

Today, enthusiasts have embraced the use of cocktail onions in other savory drinks, such as the Bloody Mary and the Bull Shot.

If you're intrigued by what a cocktail onion may be able to add to your bartending, consider making your own. This not only strips out all of the preservatives in the commercially available ones, it will also allow you to tailor the flavor to your personal taste, the season, or a specific occasion. Consider these charmed cocktail onion options: spicy (use fresh chili peppers such as jalapeños, habaneros, or ají amarillo), citrus (add a few strips of lemon, orange, or even blood orange peel, making sure to remove the pith), or herbal (a few sprigs of lavender and rosemary will work wonders).

CUCUMBERS

Cucumbers are especially easy to form into all manner of fun garnishes, as seen in the following constructions.

Rose: Using a vegetable peeler or paring knife, slice the cucumber lengthwise to create thin ribbons. Roll one end to a tight center. Keep turning the ribbon around the center until reaching the end of the ribbon. Secure with a cocktail pick and add a

cherry tomato, olive, or sprigs of dill for further decoration.

Tree: Slice the cucumber into ribbons, then loop the ribbons back and forth on a toothpick, tapering the "tree branches" from wider to narrower as you approach the "top" of the tree. Add a tiny olive or kernel of pickled corn as a trunk, or use beet strings to form a kind of maypole. Place in the glass or perch on the rim.

Waffle Cut: Score a peeled cucumber and then use a crinkle cut-knife or a mandoline to cut the cucumber into ridged wheels. These can be floated in a drink, perched on the rim of a glass, or skewered with olives.

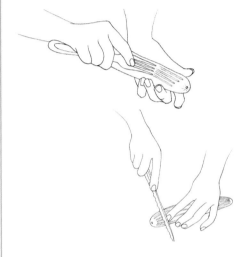

Ship: Cut three or four cucumber ribbons into triangles. Stack all but one of the triangles and then use the last triangle as a sail.

VERDANT GREEN JANGALA

Jangala is Sanskrit for jungle, and the minty, chocolate flavor of this Grasshopper remix is as beguiling and bewitching as the bounty of tropical flora and fauna.

1¹/₂ oz. green crème de menthe

1¹/₂ oz. white crème de cacao or white chocolate syrup

1¹/₂ oz. milk, cream, or cream of coconut

3 to 5 dashes of Fee Brothers Aztec Chocolate Bitters

Place all of the ingredients in a cocktail shaker filled with ice and shake vigorously.

Pour the contents of the shaker into a cordial, liqueur, or sherry glass.

FINISHING TOUCHES

Garnish with a key lime basket filled with pomegranate seeds (see pages 76–77). Or, if you prefer, cut up pieces of a colorful, soft tropical fruit such as mango or papaya to fill the basket. Key limes are small enough for the basket to perch on the glass's rim if you make an incision on the bottom. You can also place a toothpick in the underside of the basket so that it rests on the rim.

BOTANICAL GARDEN SPRITZ

For five days in May, Christmas comes to Chelsea in London—in the form of the Royal Horticultural Society's Chelsea Flower Show. With the show attended by members of the British royal family and people from all continents, the neighborhood becomes swarmed by flower enthusiasts. With their love of freshness in mind, Calum crafted this cocktail for those in town for the show.

Calum O'Flynn, bartender at The Botanist at Sloane Square, London

3/4 oz. Bloom Gin

3/4 oz. Belsazar White Vermouth

3/4 oz. Kamm & Sons British Aperitif

1/4 oz. St-Germain

4 drops of Dr. Adam Elmegirab's Dandelion and Burdock Bitters

2 oz. soda water

Place all of the ingredients in a cocktail shaker filled with ice and shake vigorously.

Strain into an ice-filled white wine glass or Nick & Nora glass.

FINISHING TOUCHES

Garnish with a long cucumber twist, a sprig of dill, and pansies. You can even throw in a cleaned peacock feather for added panache.

FULL NETTLE JACKET

This drink epitomizes May in England. The pisco provides some sunshine; St-Germain and cucumber are duly delicate; and the nettle cordial and lemon juice help keep the inevitable rain showers from getting you under the weather. The original name was "Peruvian Spring," but a friend lent Calum a pun that he couldn't resist putting on a menu.

Calum O'Flynn, bartender at The Botanist at Sloane Square, London

1¾ oz. Macchu La Diablada Pisco	Place all of the ingredients in a crystal highball glass, add crushed ice, and stir until combined.
¼ oz. St-Germain	Top with additional crushed ice.
2 oz. nettle cordial	
½ oz. fresh lemon juice	**FINISHING TOUCHES**
½ oz. cucumber syrup	Garnish with a long cucumber twist that winds throughout the glass and then add a lemon twist.

For nettle cordial: Place 4 cups of water, 1½ oz. nettles, and 1 teaspoon citric acid in a saucepan and boil until the mixture has reduced by half. Strain, add sugar in a 2:1 ratio to the resulting liquid, and stir until dissolved.

For cucumber syrup: Peel, chop, and mash a cucumber and place it in a large mason jar. Top with 3 cups simple syrup and let stand for up 24 to 36 hours. Strain, stir in 1 oz. white rum, and store in the refrigerator up to 6 months.

EARL OF HARLEM

This cocktail takes its name from the Earl Grey tea utilized in the cocktail and from the unofficial Earl of Harlem: Sean Combs, the face of Cîroc Vodka. The drink was constructed as a reproach to the bevy of sparkling cocktails that were on menus just to keep people from complaining. The delicate sweetness of prosecco works wonderfully with the rich flavors of sweet vermouth and bergamot.

Calum O'Flynn, bartender at The Botanist at Sloane Square, London

---

3/4 oz. Cîroc Vodka

1/2 oz. Mondino Amaro

1/2 oz. Belsazar Red Vermouth

1 oz. Earl Grey tea, at room temperature

2 drops of 18.21 Earl Grey Bitters

3 1/2 oz. prosecco

Place all of the ingredients, except for the prosecco, in a mixing glass filled with ice and stir until chilled.

Strain into a coupe and top with prosecco.

FINISHING TOUCHES
Fashion an orange peel flower (see page 77) and burn the edges with a match or lighter. Float the flower in the cocktail or rest it on the rim of the glass. If you're swinging past the florist before the party, an actual rose—orange or red—will also do the trick.

WHAT'S UP, DOC?

This is the first cocktail that Jelani created for the cocktail menu at Clover Club, and the carrot-greens garnish definitely utilizes the philosophy that Jelani tries to keep in mind when dreaming up a new concoction: "You drink with your eyes first."

Jelani Johnson, bartender at Clover Club, New York

---

2 oz. black currant–infused rum

¾ oz. fresh lemon juice

¾ oz. carrot juice

½ oz. orange juice

¼ oz. ginger syrup (see page 34)

¼ oz. maple syrup

dash of Dale DeGroff's Pimento Aromatic Bitters

Place all of the ingredients in a cocktail shaker filled with ice and shake vigorously.

Strain into a pilsner glass filled with crushed ice.

FINISHING TOUCHES
Garnish with a bunch of freshly washed carrot greens.

For black currant–infused rum: Place 1 cup of currants and a 750 ml bottle of Flor de Caña 7 Year or Dos Maderas 5+5 PX rum in a large mason jar and let stand for 3 days. Strain back into the bottle.

LET'S MAKE IT INTERESTING

This spring-into-summer cocktail incorporates the flavors and aromas of a blooming garden. Light and crisp with undertones of grassy sencha tea, fruity strawberry, floral rose, and bright rhubarb, it's an incredibly broad-minded drink—right down to the addition of champagne, which makes it socially acceptable to enjoy before noon.

Josh Suchan, beverage director at Skylight Gardens and founder of Ice and Alchemy, Los Angeles

1 oz. infused vodka

1/2 oz. Aperol

1/2 oz. fresh lemon juice

1/4 oz. simple syrup

champagne, to top

Place all of the ingredients, except for the champagne, in a cocktail shaker filled with ice and shake vigorously.

Strain into a chilled coupe and top with the champagne.

FINISHING TOUCHES
Float a single rose petal in the cocktail.

For infused vodka: Place 1/4 oz. strawberry sencha tea and 1 drop of rose water in a 750 ml bottle of vodka and steep for 30 minutes before straining back into the bottle.

CHERRY BLOSSOM COCKTAIL

Sakura cherry blossoms are one of the enduring symbols of Japan. Not only are they beautiful, they also have a subtle almond flavor which can be enjoyed on various confections, in a pot of rice, or pickled in a blend of salt and plum vinegar. Here, they lend their elegant appearance and taste to this cocktail.

1 oz. cherry brandy

1 oz. brandy

1/4 teaspoon curaçao

1/4 teaspoon fresh lemon juice

1/4 teaspoon grenadine

Place all of the ingredients in a cocktail shaker filled with ice and shake vigorously.

Strain into a coupe.

FINISHING TOUCHES
You can float fresh or pickled cherry blossoms (see page 109) on top of the drink. For added drama, wrap a pickled cherry blossom in its own leaf (which is also edible) and spear with a cocktail pick that has a knot of lime peel (see page 76) affixed to the far end.

ROSA PICANTE MARGARITA

Looking to dress up a jalapeño-centered Margarita, Jordan used a rose petal and a dash of rose water to balance the cocktail's heat. His simple, flowery take paid off—this cocktail was Patrón's Margarita of the Year in 2016.

Jordan Corney, bar manager at Bohanan's, San Antonio

pink Himalayan salt, for the rim

2 oz. Patrón Silver tequila

½ oz. Patrón Citrónge Lime

1 oz. fresh lime juice

½ oz. ginger syrup (see page 34)

1 barspoon of jalapeño oil

dash of rose water

Wet the rim of a chilled coupe and dip half of it into the salt.

Place all of the remaining ingredients, except for the rose water, in a cocktail shaker filled with ice and shake vigorously.

Strain the cocktail into the rimmed coupe and top with the rose water.

FINISHING TOUCHES
Garnish with a rose petal and a slice of jalapeño pepper.

PURPLE HERBAL HAZE

The color purple is associated with royalty, nobility, and luxury. Capitalize on these lofty connections with an elegant purple-hued cocktail that bursts with the freshness and vitality of a warm spring day. Crème de violette was hard to find for many years in the United States, but the recent cocktail renaissance has ushered a number of quality brands into the marketplace.

3 to 5 oz. rosé

1½ oz. crème de violette

½ oz. cognac

Place the ingredients in a champagne flute and gently stir.

FINISHING TOUCHES

Float a sprig of fresh-cut lavender, a blueberry, or a blackberry in the drink. If you're looking to really emphasize the purple quality of the drink, tie curls of purple ribbon onto a cocktail pick or float candied violets on the cocktail's surface.

For candied violets: Clip the stems from 25 violets, leaving enough that you can easily hold the blossoms while dipping them. Combine a dash of lemon juice or vodka and 1 egg white in a bowl and beat until frothy. Put 2 tablespoons powdered sugar in a sifter. Dip a violet blossom into the egg white mixture, shake off any excess, and then twirl the stem between your thumb and index finger as you evenly coat the blossom with sugar from the sifter. Place the coated violets on paper towels and repeat until they are all coated. Place in the refrigerator, uncovered, for 24 hours. Remove and let stand at room temperature for another 24 hours. Snip off stems entirely before using as garnish.

BLACK VIOLET

The Black Violet is balanced across the flavor spectrum, simple and surprising with hints of sweetness. It was created to show off the floral brightness of Hennessy Black, a decidedly different style of cognac. The lemon twist garnish helps brighten the nose and plays nicely off the crème de violette.

Jordan Bushell, national brand ambassador for Hennessy

2 oz. Hennessy Black Cognac

¼ oz. crème de violette

splash of fresh lemon juice

Place all of the ingredients in a cocktail shaker filled with ice and shake vigorously.

Strain into a chilled coupe.

FINISHING TOUCHES

Garnish with a lemon twist and an edible violet.

ARUBA ARIBA

The national cocktail of Aruba features some exotic ingredients. Coecoei, which was first made by the locals, has a distinctive red color that comes from the sap of the kukwisa, an agave plant native to the island. Pisang Ambon, a gecko-green Dutch liqueur made from a recipe with roots in Indonesia, carries a strong banana flavor with herbal notes. Garnish with a hibiscus blossom, and you've got a cocktail that is perfect for summer sipping.

1/2 oz. vodka

1/2 oz. 151-proof rum (Palmera 151 or Ron Rico 151 preferred)

1/8 oz. Coecoei

1/8 oz. Pisang Ambon liqueur

1/2 cup orange juice

1/2 cup cranberry juice

1/2 cup pineapple juice

splash of grenadine

splash of Grand Marnier

Add the ingredients to a mixing glass filled with ice in the order they are listed and then stir gently.

Pour the contents of the glass into a highball glass.

FINISHING TOUCHES
Top with a red hibiscus flower and wedge of lime skewered on an ornamental pick. If you're after additional color, a cherry and an orange wheel can serve as additional garnishes.

ANCHO ESTRELLA

Ancho is truly the estrella ("star") of this cocktail. The heart-shaped, dried version of the ripe poblano pepper, their sweet, slightly smoky flavor forms the basis of Ancho Reyes liqueur.

¼ oz. Ancho Reyes

½ oz. Dolin Vermouth de Chambéry Rouge

¼ oz. St-Germain

2 dashes of Fee Brothers Cherry Bitters

Place all of the ingredients in a cocktail shaker filled with ice and shake vigorously.

Strain into a chilled cocktail glass or coupe, or over ice in a colored mason jar.

FINISHING TOUCHES

Perch a fresh red poblano pepper on the rim of your glass, and feel free to add a shishito pepper for color, texture, and taste. If you are looking to reduce the spice, garnish with a lime wheel or Homemade Maraschino Cherry (see page 113).

CUATRO UVAS

Balancing the tart quality of lime against St-Germain, the sweet elderflower liqueur, and celery bitters brings out the best qualities in pisco. Cucamelons, one of the garnish options, are grape-sized fruits that resemble a watermelon and taste like a slightly sour cucumber.

Fabiano Latham, beverage director for Chotto Matte, London

4 red grapes

2 drops of Fee Brothers Celery Bitters

1/2 oz. fresh lime juice

1 oz. Macchu La Diablada Pisco

1 oz. honjozo sake

1 oz. St-Germain

Place the grapes and bitters in a cocktail shaker and muddle. Add ice and the remaining ingredients and shake vigorously. Strain into a chilled Hurricane glass.

FINISHING TOUCHES
If using cucamelons, cut a handful in half and drop them into the glass. If you want to keep things simple, cut a wheel from a pickling cucumber.

VARIATION
For an extra-special alternative, combine 1 cup of yuzu sake and 1 cup sugar and stir until the sugar has dissolved. Cut cucamelons in half, place them in the syrup, and let them marinate overnight. This garnish is also a terrific alternative to a lemon twist in a Martini.

ENGLISH ROSE

While sipping tea with her family, Valentina got the urge to capture the serene beauty of an English rose garden on a summer's day. Dedicated to her beloved uncle and his breathtaking garden, the gin-based English Rose proves that her aim is true.

Valentina Carbone, bartender at Nobu Berkeley St, London

2 oz. gin

1 oz. rose syrup

1 oz. yuzu juice

1 barspoon of Chartreuse

1 slice of lemon

1 slice of lime

1 slice of grapefruit

1 strawberry

2 blueberries

2 raspberries

Place all of the ingredients in a cocktail shaker filled with ice and shake vigorously.

Strain into a cocktail glass.

FINISHING TOUCHES
Garnish with an edible rose petal or two.

For rose syrup: Place equal parts rose water and sugar in a saucepan and bring to a boil, while stirring, until the sugar has dissolved. Let cool and store in the refrigerator for up to 1 month.

CHANDON PINKALICIOUS

Hibiscus lends its charm to kombucha and ice cubes in this bubbly cocktail. Its taste and lovely pink hue are certain to melt your heart.

Courtesy of Chandon

1½ oz. hibiscus kombucha

½ oz. limoncello

3 drops of Fee Brothers Rhubarb Bitters

2 oz. Chandon Rosé

Pour the kombucha, limoncello, and bitters in a champagne flute and top with rosé.

FINISHING TOUCHES
Add hibiscus-blossom ice cubes to your glass and garnish with a hibiscus flower.

For hibiscus-blossom ice cubes: Fill the bottom third of each mold in an ice cube tray with water. Place 1 to 2 edible hibiscus blossoms and place in the freezer until set. Fill the remainder of each mold with water and return to freezer until set.

CHANDON PINK PUNCH

There are times when you can never have too much Chandon Pinkalicious at hand. This punch, which calls for an entire bottle, is for those moments.

Courtesy of Chandon

---

2 cups hibiscus kombucha

¹/₂ cup limoncello

16 drops of Fee Brothers Rhubarb Bitters

1 (750 ml) bottle of Chandon Rosé

Place the kombucha, limoncello, and bitters into a large punch bowl, stir, and add ice.

Top with the bottle of rosé and serve.

FINISHING TOUCHES
Place hibiscus-blossom ice cubes (see page 183) in your glass. Or fill a Bundt pan with water and hibiscus blossoms, freeze until set, and add to the punch bowl.

SWEETS

When it comes down to it, everyone's open to the whimsy and excitement that candy and confections can add to a cocktail. From Cracker Jacks and Reese's Peanut Butter Cups to jelly beans, peanut brittle, candy corn, and candy canes, the trip back to the simpler times of childhood will be welcomed by all when deployed smartly.

While candy garnishes work best on specific occasions such as Christmas, Valentine's Day, Halloween, engagement parties, weddings, and anniversaries, don't shy away from using candy whenever the mood strikes—because, deep down, we all have an incorrigible sweet tooth.

Whether you're channeling Willy Wonka or renowned pastry chef Jacques Torres, creamier drinks, like Chocolate Martinis or a White Russian, can easily accommodate a rim coated with agave, honey, or simple syrup and rolled in chocolate shavings. Crushed nuts make a delicious companion to the chocolate rim, bringing that beloved sweet-and-savory combination to the cocktail world.

For winter-themed cocktails, you can rim the glass with melted white chocolate before dipping it into crushed peppermint candies, caramel, or mint. For an ice cream parlor dream, coat the rim of the glass in rainbow or chocolate sprinkles and garnish with a Homemade Maraschino Cherry (see page 113).

Fresh whipped cream is also a hallmark of sweet drinks. Infuse the whipped cream with herbs, both savory and sweet, to add a bit of bliss to any creamy or fruity cocktail.

Tiki cocktails are a home for toasted candied coconut, and they're even outgoing enough to permit a colorful Peep on the rim. If marshmallow is not your thing, the colorful sugar that makes the Peep pop can be added to the rim to draw out elements of the cocktail and seduce your guests.

The rainbow of colors that licorice is available in make it a go-to candy garnish. It can be placed directly in the glass to enhance the cocktail's visual elements, used as a swizzle stick, or, if you're using shoelace licorice, draped over the rim and tied into a bow or woven into a spiderweb to capture the drinker's imagination. You can use caramel, applied to a glass before it is put into the freezer, to achieve a similarly delicate effect.

A simple but delightful way to utilize candy in cocktail making is to skewer two or three of your favorite bites and drop it into the cocktail.

Gummy candies can be infused with alcohol to boost the strength and taste of any beverage, and citrus-flavored candies can be paired with a fruit garnish.

Think of candy garnishes as you would a potential partner—a little boldness and a bit of sweetness goes a long way.

KAFI TRÄSCH

This Swiss take on the Irish Coffee is terrific at the end of a meal, with brunch, or during late-night cocktail parties. Traditionally, the drink requires thin—as in not strong—coffee. But I suggest using a robust, flavorful joe that can stand up to the schnapps and sugar. Träsch, plum schnapps, or kirsch are standard, but this cocktail works with almost any variety of schnapps.

½ oz. hot water	Add the ingredients to an Irish Coffee glass in the order they are listed.
2 to 3 sugar cubes	
¼ oz. träsch	Stir until the mixture resembles a light tea. If using regular coffee, the coloration will be slightly darker.
a few grains of Nescafé or other instant coffee	

Cocktails of the World

As I graduated from a school in Lucerne, Switzerland has always been a kind of dreamland for me, perhaps because the Alps place you that much closer to heaven. I adored Kafi Träsch during my time there, and, while it is lovely any time, it is particularly perfect as a warm refreshment on the ski slopes.

KAFI LUZ

This take on the Kafi Träsch is meant to be tailored to your own personal taste, so don't be afraid to indulge your personal cravings when selecting schnapps for the mix.

½ oz. hot water

½ teaspoon Nescafé or other coffee

2 to 3 sugar cubes

¼ oz. preferred schnapps mix (a mix of plum and pear schnapps, or elderberry and mint, for example)

Add the ingredients to an Irish Coffee glass in the order they are listed.

Stir until the mixture resembles a light tea. If using regular coffee, the coloration will be slightly darker.

VARIATION: KAFI PFLÜMLI
Follow the same instructions as above but use plum schnapps in place of the mixture. This is the most popular variation.

VARIATION: KAFI KIRSCH
Follow the same instructions as above, using kirsch (cherry schnapps) in place of the mixture.

My favorite variation of the Kafi Träsch is the Grääm version, which adds cream or whipped cream to the above recipes.

A LONG NIGHT IN MADRID

Madeira is a fortified wine that is heated while it rests in the barrel to replicate the hot conditions seen on ships in the port of Madeira centuries ago. The resultant roasted notes pair nicely with maple syrup and Angostura bitters, drawing out the spicy and oaky qualities of the wine and balancing the cognac. The egg white provides body and lightens a cocktail filled with rich flavors.

Jordan Bushell, national brand ambassador for Hennessy

1¹/₂ oz. Hennessy V.S

³/₄ oz. Madeira

¹/₄ oz. grade A maple syrup

4 dashes of Angostura bitters

1 egg white

Place the ingredients in a cocktail shaker with no ice and dry shake.

Add ice and shake until chilled.

Strain into a coupe or cocktail glass.

FINISHING TOUCHES

For a wonderful, subtle touch, grate a cacao nib or a piece of dark chocolate over the cocktail.

LA DIABLADA

The miniature brownie is a perfect complement to this sweet, herbal cocktail. The name, which translates as "the devil's dance," stems from a traditional bolero in Puno, Peru.

Isaac Morrison, drink consultant at Dash Concept

½ oz. Agwa de Bolivia (coca leaf liqueur) or other herbal syrup

¾ oz. Macchu La Diablada Pisco

½ oz. pineapple juice

½ oz. fresh lime juice

½ oz. Aperol

Cava (or preferred sparkling wine), to top

Place all of the ingredients, except the sparkling wine, in a cocktail shaker filled with ice and shake vigorously.

Strain into a champagne flute and top with the sparkling wine.

FINISHING TOUCHES
Place a small brownie skewered on a curved bamboo stick or cocktail pick directly into the glass.

VIKING'S LITTLE MERMAID

The Little Mermaid statue at the Langelinie promenade in Copenhagen is Denmark's icon. This glamorous gal, who was commissioned by the owners of the Carlsberg brewery and inspired by the Hans Christian Andersen fairy tale, provides this cocktail's moniker.

cherry syrup, for the rim

ginger sugar, for the rim

¼ oz. aquavit

¼ oz. Peter Heering Cherry Liqueur

½ oz. Dansk Danish Red Lager (or preferred "red" beer)

¼ oz. Strongbow Cherry Blossom hard cider

splash of Luxardo maraschino liqueur or liquid from Homemade Maraschino Cherries (see page 113)

1 oz. fresh lemon juice

Wet the rim of a snifter with the cherry syrup and dip it into the ginger sugar.

Place the remaining ingredients in a cocktail shaker filled with ice and shake vigorously.

Place ice in the snifter and strain the cocktail into the glass.

FINISHING TOUCHES

Garnish with red shoelace licorice, which amplifies the taste of the aquavit! Top with a Luxardo maraschino cherry, and a slice of ginger or orange. Consider accessorizing with a plastic mermaid (these can be found as cupcake toppers) lounging on the rim of the glass.

For cherry syrup: Add 2 tablespoons of liquid from a jar of Luxardo maraschino cherries to a standard simple syrup once the sugar has dissolved. Stir to combine, remove from heat, and let cool before storing in the refrigerator.

For ginger sugar: Preheat the oven to 200°F. Combine ¼ cup demerara sugar and 1 tablespoon grated ginger and place the mixture on a baking sheet. Bake until the mixture just starts to melt, about 5 minutes. Remove and let stand until dry, approximately 2 days.

Cocktails of the World

In Denmark, the *velkomst-drink*, or welcome drink, is served shortly after guests arrive.

THE AVIATION ADAPTATION

First published in 1916, the recipe for the Aviation evolved as time marched on. The original called for gin, lemon juice, maraschino liqueur, and crème de violette, which lent the cocktail a sky-blue tint that set wondrous visions of planes in flight drifting through the minds of those who encountered it. This is Josh's modest deconstruction, garnished with a crème de violette cloud that dissolves in the drink to match the enchanting tint of the original.

Josh Suchan, beverage director at Skylight Gardens and founder of Ice and Alchemy, Los Angeles

2 oz. London Dry gin

3/4 oz. fresh lemon juice

1/2 oz. Luxardo maraschino liqueur

1/4 oz. crème de violette

Place the ingredients in a cocktail shaker filled with ice and shake vigorously.

Strain into a chilled cocktail glass or coupe.

FINISHING TOUCHES

Garnish with a maraschino cherry that has a lemon twist wrapped around it, or use a crème de violette cloud. If you're going to make the crème de violette cloud, you will need a cotton candy machine. Add crème de violette to 2 tablespoons purple floss sugar until the mixture resembles wet sand. Add 2 dashes of Scrappy's Lavender Bitters. Mix until thoroughly combined, and let the mixture harden overnight. Once hardened, break into smaller pieces and place them into a cotton candy machine. Spin into cotton candy according to manufacturer's directions.

PISCO PARADISE

With the first sip, the drinker gets the aroma of the pisco, then the mellow, nutty flavor of quinoa, and finally the pleasant bitterness of cacao. Isaac is focused on far more than aesthetics when he considers a garnish, saying: "The garnish should look beautiful, of course, but at the same time, it should also bring some sort of unexpected surprise that adds to the drinking experience."

Isaac Morrison, drink consultant at Dash Concept

3/4 oz. quinoa juice

1/2 oz. cacao leaf–infused pisco

3/4 oz. fresh lime juice

3/4 oz. honey syrup (see page 85)

Place the ingredients in a cocktail shaker filled with ice and shake vigorously.

Strain into a coupe.

FINISHING TOUCHES
Top with egg-white foam. To make, place ice, 1 egg white, and 1 1/2 oz. white cocoa syrup in a cocktail shaker and shake until frothy. After adding the foam to the cocktail, sprinkle cacao powder and Peruvian pink salt on top.

For quinoa juice: Place 2 cups apple juice, 4 cups water, 4 tablespoons quinoa, and 2 cinnamon sticks in a saucepan and bring to a boil. Reduce heat to low and simmer for 15 to 20 minutes. Remove from heat, let cool, strain, and store in the refrigerator.

For cacao leaf-infused pisco: Place 2 cacao leaves in 1 cup of pisco and let stand until desired flavor has been achieved. Remove leaves before using.

Cocktails of the World

A large natural salt reserve lies outside of Cuzco, Peru. It was the main salt supply for the Incan Empire and is one of the only spots outside of the Himalayas that naturally produces pink salt.

NUTTY, SMOKY, AND MEATY

Nuts are the hard-shelled fruits of plants. But when it comes to a cocktail party, strict taxonomy is to be left on the shelf. For example, peanuts are not a nut but a legume. Almonds, pistachios, and cashews are also not nuts but fruit seeds. Other seeds, such as sunflower and pumpkin, aren't considered nuts, but they will provide nutty flavor to any preparation they pop up in.

Nutmeg is another nut impostor. Made from the seeds of the nutmeg tree, this fragrant and delicious flavoring can be found in numerous drink recipes. In high doses, nutmeg has been reported to be a hallucinogen, but when sprinkled over a libation it lives up to its reputation as a soothing balm. For centuries, various cultures added nutmeg to warm milk to help induce sleep, aid digestion, and relieve pain. The popularity of the Painkiller, a beloved rum cocktail, relies heavily on the inclusion of nutmeg.

For stronger cocktails, consider using whole, crushed, smoked, shaved, or ground almonds, hazelnuts, cashews, pistachios, and seeds as a garnish. Drop them into the drink; use them to rim a glass; or spear a few on a cocktail pick. Macadamia nuts and walnuts both pair nicely with any cocktail that utilizes Fee Brothers Black Walnut Bitters.

Another favorite garnish, the coconut, takes center stage in summertime favorites and tiki drinks. The word *coconut* is derived from the sixteenth-century Portuguese and Spanish word *cocos*, meaning "grinning face," because the three small holes on its shell resemble human facial features. The coconut might be the king of confusing classification: it's considered a fruit, a nut, and a seed. Leaving that identity crisis alone, the coconut can be used as a drinking vessel, as a floating garnish, or, shredded, to rim a fruity cocktail. As if its good looks and versatility weren't enough, try garnishing your next Piña Colada with Coconut Curls. To make Coconut Curls, bake a whole coconut in the oven for 10 minutes. Remove, let cool, and split with a hammer. Remove the flesh and, using a very sharp knife, cut into very thin strands about 4" to 6" long. Hang off the rim of a glass for an elegant, languid look.

MEATY AND SMOKY

Garnishing with meat—whether lamb, chorizo, or beef—is a great option with savory drinks like the Bloody Mary and the Bull Shot, as well as cocktails based on beer, bourbon, or Scotch. Cocktails featuring sake are another good spot to beef up your garnish game, since the rice-and-meat pairing is tried and true. Combining meat with umami-laden items like mushrooms, olives, tomatoes, or Parmesan cheese is another way to dress for success.

Washing spirits with sausage, bacon, or oxtail imparts a smoky and savory kick to each sip. To make meaty mixers, cook the meat in a cold pan to render the fat. Add the drippings to your chosen liquor (bourbon and gin work especially well) and freeze until the fat separates and sits in a hardened layer on top. Remove the layer of fat and start dreaming up ways to make use of the rich flavor.

ORGEAT

While you can purchase orgeat, you can also readily make this classic French syrup, which is a key component in a number of tropical drinks.

2 cups raw almonds

1 to 1½ cups simple syrup

1 teaspoon rose water or orange blossom water

2 oz. vodka

Preheat the oven to 400°F.

Place the almonds on a baking sheet and toast in the oven for 5 minutes. Remove and let cool.

Once cool, pulverize the nuts in a food processor, blender, or grain mill.

Prepare the simple syrup. When it is hot and the sugar has dissolved, add the almond meal and remove the pan from heat. Let the mixture stand for 3 to 6 hours.

Strain the mixture through cheesecloth and discard the solids.

Add the rose water or orange blossom water and the vodka. Stir to combine and store in the refrigerator for up to 3 weeks.

I'M NUTTY FOR YOU

This is a poke at the Reverend Sylvester Graham, whose tireless preaching about the ills of alcohol—and all forms of delight—inspired the creation of graham flour. Unfortunately for the good reverend, graham crackers go wonderfully with a number of libations.

honey, for the rim

graham cracker crumbs, for the rim

1/2 oz. Best Damn Cherry Cola

1/4 oz. Lapsang souchong & vanilla syrup (see page 122)

1/4 oz. gin

1/4 oz. Amaro Averna

2 to 3 dashes of Fee Brothers Black Walnut Bitters

Coat the rim of an Old Fashioned glass with the honey and dip it into the graham cracker crumbs.

Place the remaining ingredients in a cocktail shaker filled with ice and shake vigorously.

Place ice in the glass and strain the cocktail into it.

FINISHING TOUCHES
Skewer Cracker Jacks on a toothpick or cocktail pick. For a fancier touch, garnish with a speared maraschino cherry and float a star anise pod in the glass.

OPEN SÉSAME

A key ingredient in this drink, which is named for the magical phrase in the story "Ali Baba and the Forty Thieves," is tahini, a sesame seed paste that possesses a rich yet delicate nutty flavor that will uncover some elements that you never suspected to be hidden away in tequila and rum.

1 oz. añejo tequila

1½ oz. rum

¼ oz. crème de cacao

½ oz. chocolate syrup

½ oz. cream

½ oz. coconut milk

½ oz. tahini

Place the tequila, rum, and crème de cacao in a cocktail shaker and stir to combine. Add ice and the remaining ingredients and shake vigorously.

Strain into a chilled Old Fashioned glass or a coupe.

FINISHING TOUCHES
Place ½ oz. of cream and the spring from a Hawthorne strainer in a cocktail shaker. Shake until the cream is frothy and pour it on top of the cocktail. Sprinkle with toasted coconut and either harissa powder or another spice blend, such as La Boite's Za'atar (a blend of sesame, sumac, thyme, and oregano) or Tangier (rose petals, cumin, and cardamom; see pages 36–37).

SMOKY BOURBON & GINGER COCKTAIL

There's no denying the decadent charm of America's national spirit: bourbon. The Lapsang souchong & vanilla syrup works overtime here, amplifying the spirit's spicy fragrance and enhancing the vanilla and caramel notes it is legendary for. Artisanal, high-quality ginger ale is also key, as it is strong and spicy enough to stand up to the potent flavor of bourbon.

1/2 oz. small batch bourbon (such as Jefferson's or Willett's Pot Still Reserve)

3/4 oz. natural, craft ginger ale

2 to 3 barspoons Lapsang souchong & vanilla syrup (see page 122)

Place all of the ingredients in a cocktail shaker filled with ice and shake vigorously.

Strain into an Old Fashioned glass filled with ice or into a chilled coupe.

FINISHING TOUCHES
Garnish with candied ginger and two Homemade Maraschino Cherries (see page 113).

EL VIEJO

"Pisco, Peru's national spirit, is distilled from grapes and overwhelmingly associated with the Pisco Sour. This well-known shaken cocktail is a delicious and refreshing tipple made with pisco, citrus, sugar, egg white, and bitters," says the talented Josh Suchan. "I wanted to fully explore pisco's unique flavor profiles, so I came up with an Old Fashioned variation focusing on the nutty, bready, cognac-like qualities of the Quebranta grape varietal in combination with cacao, pecans, and a lemon twist."

**Josh Suchan, beverage director at Skylight Gardens
and founder of Ice and Alchemy, Los Angeles**

2¹/₂ oz. Pisco Huamaní Quebranta

1 teaspoon Tempus Fugit Crème de Cacao

¹/₂ teaspoon simple syrup

3 dashes of Miracle Mile Toasted Pecan Bitters

dash of Angostura bitters

Place all of the ingredients in a mixing glass filled with ice and stir for 30 seconds or until properly chilled and diluted.

Place an ice sphere in a mason jar or other large glass. At home, you can use round ice molds or freeze water in bowls in order to create the sphere.

Strain the cocktail into the glass.

FINISHING TOUCHES
Express a strip of lemon zest over the cocktail and then drop the now-twisted peel into the cocktail. Fill a food smoker with medium-bodied cigar tobacco and then insert the tool's hose into the jar, just above the cocktail. Fill the remaining space in the jar with smoke. Seal the jar for a moment and open it to release the smoke and wow your guests. The intensity of the tobacco flavor will increase the longer the smoke remains in the jar.

ASHES TO ASHES

Dark and foreboding in appearance and yet bursting with flavor, this drink was named for the activated charcoal it contains and for the contemplative manner it encourages. It is a drink to sit with at the end of the evening, allowing the drink to reveal more and more of itself. Don't be scared off by the charcoal—it does not have any flavor, and the dramatic effect it produces is not to be missed.

Jordan Bushell, national brand ambassador for Hennessy

1¹/₂ oz. Hennessy V.S

1 oz. 10-year-old tawny port

¹/₂ teaspoon activated charcoal

2 dashes of Fee Brothers Aztec Chocolate Bitters

Place all of the ingredients in a mixing glass filled with ice and stir until chilled.

Pour into an Old Fashioned glass.

FINISHING TOUCHES
Drop a Luxardo maraschino cherry, or a Homemade Maraschino Cherry (see page 113), and a red rose petal into the cocktail.

CUZCO MARTINI

Award-winning mixologist Valentina Carbone is a true Renaissance woman, all the way down to her Italian heritage. She put her considerable knowledge to good use in this homage to Cuzco, Peru's ancient capital. By balancing the pisco with spicy jalapeño and fragrant rosemary and adding a showstopping garnish of black truffle and grilled beef heart, Valentina created a cocktail that is as well-rounded as she is.

Valentina Carbone, bartender at Nobu Berkeley St, London

1 slice of green jalapeño pepper

$1/2$ oz. agave nectar

1 sprig of rosemary

$1/2$ oz. fresh lemon juice

2 oz. pisco

3 drops of truffle oil

Place the jalapeño and the agave nectar in a cocktail shaker and muddle.

Add ice and the remaining ingredients and shake vigorously.

Strain into a cocktail glass.

FINISHING TOUCHES
Place a slice of black truffle on the surface of the cocktail. Skewer the grilled beef heart with a toothpick and rest it on the side of the glass.

SHISO SMOKIN'

"This drink came to me while I just was getting over a bout of tonsillitis and was trying to drink all things ginger," Fabiano says. "This is a Japanese riff on the Penicillin, which was invented at Milk & Honey in New York by bartender Sam Ross."

Fabiano Latham, beverage director for Chotto Matte, London

1 shiso leaf

1¼ oz. Japanese malt whisky

½ oz. yuzu sake

⅔ oz. fresh lemon juice

⅓ oz. rich ginger syrup

⅓ oz. Lapsang souchong syrup

Crumple the shiso leaf and place it in a cocktail shaker. Add ice and the remaining ingredients and shake vigorously.

Strain over a large ice cube in a chilled Old Fashioned glass.

FINISHING TOUCHES
Place 1 cup of Islay Scotch—a heavily peated whisky with a luxurious tobacco-y finish—and 2 teaspoons of Lapsang souchong tea in a mason jar and let steep for 1 hour. Strain into a small spritz bottle and rigorously spray in and around the drink to infuse the cocktail with the smoky aroma. You want it smelling very smoky, almost burnt. This will amplify the spice from the ginger, the citrus from the yuzu sake and lemon, the malty whisky, and the mint-basil flavor of the shiso leaf.

For rich ginger syrup: Place equal parts ginger juice and sugar in a saucepan and warm over medium heat, while stirring, until the sugar has dissolved. Remove from heat and let cool before storing in the refrigerator.

For Lapsang souchong syrup: Place equal parts strong Lapsang souchong tea and sugar in a saucepan and warm over medium heat, while stirring, until the sugar has dissolved. Remove from heat and let cool before storing in the refrigerator.

BULL SHOT

Once considered a classic "morning after" cocktail, the Bull Shot is a close cousin to the Bloody Mary, switching beef bouillon or consommé in for the tomato juice. The Detroit's Caucus Club lays claim to birthing the Bull around 1952, but it was the Hollywood set that placed the drink in the spotlight. By the end of Eisenhower's second term, the cocktail was having its moment. The Bull Shot was looked upon as a "freak drink" that—much like today's craft cocktails—required unusual ingredients. In those days, bartenders shrugged it off as a cocktail that required too much work and featured no small amount of grandstanding—which is exactly why celebrities ordered it up until the 1980s. This recipe is my twist on the now-forgotten classic.

1/2 teaspoon Worcestershire sauce

1/8 teaspoon celery salt

pinch of sea salt

pinch of freshly ground black pepper

2 dashes of Fee Brothers Black Walnut Bitters

dash of Tabasco™ or preferred hot sauce

2 oz. vodka

6 oz. chilled double-strength beef broth or beef bouillon

3 to 4 seasoned ice cubes

Place all of the ingredients, except for the seasoned ice cubes, in a cocktail shaker filled with ice and shake vigorously.

Place the seasoned ice cubes in an Old Fashioned or highball glass and strain the cocktail into the glass.

FINISHING TOUCHES

Hang a lemon or lime wedge on the rim of the glass. Garnish with celery or fennel tops, if available, and dust the top of the drink with a pinch of Sazón. You can also rim the glass with Sazón, white pepper, or ají amarillo powder before shaking the cocktail.

For seasoned ice cubes: Place 1 to 2 pounds of trimmed and chopped celery, 1 trimmed and chopped bulb of fennel (reserve some fennel or celery tops for garnish), 1 teaspoon of Sazón, 2 tablespoons of fresh lemon juice, and a pinch of seasoned salt in a blender and puree until smooth. Fill each mold in an ice cube tray halfway with the puree and top with water. Freeze until set.

Sazón is a mix of garlic and cumin
that has hints of pepper and nutmeg.

BLOODY IRISH BEEF STEW

Tom told me that when he worked Sundays at Fitzgerald's Pub in New York, more than a hundred people would come to the bar in the first 45 minutes to get one of his handmade Bloody Marys. One of those people was from Texas, and Tom made him a Bloody Bull, which is a Bloody Mary with au jus (a beef bouillon–based gravy) floated on top. The drink was such a hit that Tom now brings a bag of chipped sirloin to every Sunday brunch.

Tom Sebazco, entrepreneur and bartender at Fitzgerald's Pub, New York

salt for the rim, plus more to taste

2 oz. Long Island Spirits LiV vodka

2 oz. tomato juice

1/4 oz. fresh lemon juice

dash of Worcestershire sauce

dash of Tabasco™ sauce

freshly ground black pepper, to taste

Wet the rim of a pint glass and dip it into the salt.

Place all of the ingredients in a cocktail shaker filled with ice and shake vigorously.

Pour the contents of the shaker into the rimmed glass.

FINISHING TOUCHES
Float 1 oz. of sirloin au jus on top of drink. Place a celery stalk with its bottom directly in the drink. Skewer a cooked sirloin chip, baby carrots, a pearl onion, olives, baby potatoes, and a lemon twist with a cocktail pick. You can also just skewer the sirloin chip and place the veggies and lemon twist directly into the cocktail.

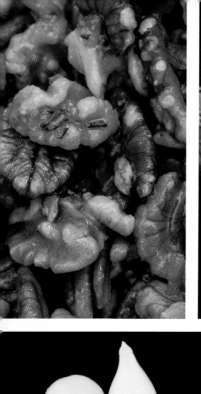

GLAMOROUS

GARNITURE

Now that homegrown and artisanal ingredients and incredible passion have raised cocktail making to the level of art, eye-catching garnishes, especially those that tell the cocktail's story, are a must. While there's never been any question about cocktails' ability to bolster a drinker's storytelling, glamorous and entertaining garnishes have long been overlooked. Think of them as the cocktail's protagonist, lending drama and intrigue to the narrative. A few of our favorite leads follow:

Edible Glitter: Life always needs a little pixie dust. Dip a glass in simple syrup and roll in edible glitter for instant glam.

Salt Air: A type of foam, salt air garnish imparts salinity and texture, not unlike sea foam. Combine 1 cup of water, 1/2 cup fresh lime juice, 1 tablespoon sea salt, and 1 tablespoon of sucrose, sucrose esters, emulsifier, or soy lecithin (though the latter doesn't create as stable a foam) in a saucepan and simmer, while stirring, over medium-low heat until the solids have dissolved. Remove from heat and whip in a blender or with a handheld mixer on high until the mixture is a thick, sturdy froth.

Painting with Bitters: Create monograms, crests, team logos, and flower petals on a drink's foam by using bitters sprayed from an oil mister. Use your favorite bitters or explore artisanal creations like those from Modern Bar Cart, whose ever-expanding collection of handcrafted bitters include chocolate, sarsaparilla, tiki, savory, and spicy varieties.

Painting with Fruit Juice: For this extension of a centuries-old technique, thicken a fruit syrup with pectin, agar agar powder, or gelatin and add the mixture to a fruit juice. Stir, adding more thickened syrup as needed, until you have a paint-like consistency. Apply to the inside of a glass in any design you want.

Lemon Ash: To balance out a frothy, sweet cocktail and inject lemony fragrance, place lemon peels in a 400°F oven and roast until they turn to charcoal, 6 to 8 hours. Place in a food processor and pulse until you have a powder. Sift to remove any large pieces and sprinkle onto the drink's surface.

Burned Citrus: For a smoky showstopper, take a piece of citrus fruit and hold it over a flame until charred. Slice the charred fruit into wheels, sprinkle with white or brown sugar, and place under the broiler until the sugar melts. You can also remove the peel and follow the same method.

Dry Ice: Lend a touch of mystery to any occasion with easy-to-procure dry ice. Place blocks of dry ice beneath a punch bowl or drop chips into a cocktail shaker after shaking the cocktail but before straining. Just make sure to handle dry ice very carefully, and never place a piece in your mouth or ingest it.

Cereal: Your favorite cereal can add a snap, crackle, and pop to creamy cocktails. Float it on top, use it to rim a glass, skewer with a swizzle stick, or pair it with tiny marshmallows and fruit. Think Cocoa Puffs and Baileys or Fruity Pebbles as a vodka infusion when you're looking to appeal to the child that lives on in every adult. For added flair, toss a decoder ring or other cereal-related prize around the glass's stem.

PISCO ROYALE

"For the launch of COYA in Miami, we wanted to create the most remarkable pisco program in the country," says Pottage. "After all, COYA was going to be the first Peruvian fine-dining restaurant with a private member's club in the U.S. Lizzie and Melanie, the owners of Macchu Pisco, were visiting us. We had a long day tasting the various cocktails and foods that were still contenders to make it into our menus. As the night waned and the entire group was toasting to the prospects ahead, Lizzie volunteered a recipe for a luxurious Pisco Sour to match the glamorous setting our team had created. Topped with Taittinger Cuvée Prestige Rosé, we had a version worthy of royalty."

Maria Pottage, beverage director at COYA Restaurant & Members Lounge, Miami

1 oz. Macchu La Diablada Pisco
½ oz. fresh key lime juice
½ oz. fresh lime juice
1 oz. simple syrup
¼ oz. Taittinger Cuvée Prestige Rosé

Place all of the ingredients, except the rosé, in a cocktail shaker with no ice and dry shake. Add ice and shake until chilled.

Strain into a chilled coupe and top with the rosé.

FINISHING TOUCHES
Place a flake of gold leaf in the center of the glass.

NEGRONI CARBONATO

This classic cocktail takes its inspiration from the Negroni Sbagliato, which is made with Campari, sweet vermouth, and sparkling wine. Presented in handcrafted copper servingware, this update is certain to turn heads.

Xavier Herit, bartender and owner of Wallflower, New York

1½ oz. Campari
1 oz. Byrrh Grand Quinquina
½ oz. Cynar
½ oz. verjus
¼ oz. lemon sorbet
1½ oz. cava
½ oz. Perrier
dash of orange bitters
1 orange peel

Place the ingredients in a 6 oz. bottle and force-carbonate using a SodaStream or a similar device. Cap immediately, do not shake or stir, and store in the refrigerator to preserve the carbonation.

FINISHING TOUCHES
Pour into an eye-catching copper container filled with crushed ice, such as the servingware traditionally used to chill the Turkish liqueur raki. An elegant wine glass will also work well here.

"Some of our regulars were planning to go back and visit Istanbul, Turkey, and had been challenging me to make a cocktail with raki, or 'Lion's Milk,' the anise-tasting liquor popular in the Mediterranean, especially Turkey, not unlike ouzo," says Xavier Herit when talking about the Negroni Carbonato. "They upped the challenge, offering to bring back some of the copper raki serving pieces. Luckily, they were able to bring ten pieces back to New York. And these raki drink coolers are heavy! Not many customers would do that for you. They definitively contributed to the success of this cocktail."

SPA DAY

This cocktail, which will serve two people, is inspired by the year Josh spent teaching English in East Asia, where tea is a daily ritual. He wanted to create a low-proof tea cocktail with detoxifying qualities that would take him back to those moments of peace and relaxation.

Josh Suchan, beverage director at Skylight Gardens
and founder of Ice and Alchemy, Los Angeles

1½ oz. honey-galangal cordial

4 oz. Moroccan tea–infused shochu

1½ oz. fresh lemon juice

Place the ingredients in a cocktail shaker filled with ice and shake vigorously.

Strain into a chilled teapot (ceramic is best).

Pour the drink into teacups.

FINISHING TOUCHES
If you want to take the tea theme a step further, place a chip of dry ice or a dry ice pellet in a stainless-steel tea ball or infuser. Place this inside the teapot to give the illusion of a piping-hot cup of tea.

For honey-galangal cordial: Place 1 cup honey and 1 cup water in a saucepan and warm over medium heat, while stirring, until the honey has dissolved. Remove pan from heat and add 3 oz. grated galangal. Let steep for at least 30 minutes, strain into a bottle, and store in the refrigerator.

For Moroccan tea–infused shochu: Place ¼ cup Moroccan tea and a 750 ml bottle of Kurouma shochu in a large mason jar and steep for 30 minutes while shaking periodically. Strain back into the shochu bottle.

HENNESSY GLITTER AND GOLD

"In most cases, the garnish on a cocktail is part of the flavor element of the drink. Gold, having no flavor, does not add to the drink in that way," Bushell explains. *"Nonetheless, I played with gold because of the human element. We taste first with our eyes, and the gold garnish sparks and delights people long before they can take their first sip."*

Jordan Bushell, national brand ambassador for Hennessy

2 oz. Hennessy V.S.O.P Privilège

2 oz. honey & clove syrup

¹/₄ oz. fresh lemon juice

dash of Hella Cocktail Co. Ginger Bitters

Place all of the ingredients in a cocktail shaker filled with ice and shake until chilled.

Strain into a coupe.

FINISHING TOUCHES
Garnish with a piece of gold leaf skewered on a green pine needle.

For honey & clove syrup: Place 1 cup honey, 1 cup water, and 10 cloves in a saucepan and bring to a boil, while stirring. When the honey has dissolved, remove from heat, let cool, and strain before storing in the refrigerator.

ALABASTER CAVERNS

"This winter menu offering is based on one of the state parks in Oklahoma," says Damon. "The milky coloring of the drink reflects the geological formations of the park, with the crushed ice mimicking the cold winters."

Damon Boelte, bartender at Grand Army, Brooklyn

1¹/₂ oz. Cutty Sark Scotch whisky

¹/₂ oz. Lustau East India Solera sherry

¹/₂ oz. cinnamon syrup

dash of Angostura bitters

¹/₂ oz. fresh lime juice

1 pineapple chunk

1 oz. coconut cream mix (1:1 ratio of coconut milk and Coco López Cream of Coconut)

Place all of the ingredients in a cocktail shaker containing 3 ice cubes and shake vigorously.

Strain over crushed ice into a pilsner glass.

FINISHING TOUCHES
Place 2 to 4 pineapple leaves in the glass so that they stick straight up.

For cinnamon syrup: Add 3 cinnamon sticks to a standard simple syrup after the sugar has dissolved. Remove from heat, let stand until cool, and remove the cinnamon sticks before storing in the refrigerator.

MAYAN VOLCANO BOWL

This large-format recipe serves two to four people and is best served in a volcano bowl (which you may recognize from various tiki cocktails), as the fire-and-nutmeg combo adds to this drink's spicy-sweetness.

Marlo Gamora, bartender at Dante NYC and Mother of Pearl, New York

3 oz. demerara rum

2 oz. Jamaican rum

1 oz. aged Trinidadian rum

1 oz. white grapefruit juice

1 oz. vanilla syrup

1/2 oz. St. Elizabeth Allspice Dram

6 dashes of Angostura bitters

1 oz. fresh lime juice

1 1/2 oz. pineapple juice

3/4 oz. 151-proof demerara rum

Place all of the ingredients, except the 151-proof rum, into a blender and pulse to combine.

Pour the blended drink mix into the volcano bowl and top with the 151-proof rum.

FINISHING TOUCHES
Place pineapple chunks along the edge of the bowl and place pineapple leaves on either side of each chunk. Before serving, light the 151-proof rum on fire and sprinkle nutmeg on top of the flames. Wait until the fire has gone out before consuming.

For vanilla syrup: Add 2 split vanilla bean pods or 1 oz. vanilla extract to a standard simple syrup after the sugar has dissolved. Remove from heat and let cool. If using vanilla bean pods, strain before storing in the refrigerator.

GAME CHANGER

"The first person I served this drink to claimed that she didn't like cognac or Scotch. She sipped this cocktail and her face took on a look of adulation for the drink in her hands. When I told her what was in it, she replied, somewhat under her breath, 'Game changer.' With a surprising combination of smoke from the Scotch, spice from Hennessy, and sweet from the pineapple, this drink is a game changer for sure," says Hennessy's Jordan Bushell.

Jordan Bushell, national brand ambassador for Hennessy

1¹/₂ oz. Hennessy V.S

¹/₄ oz. Ardbeg 10-Year-Old Scotch whisky

¹/₂ oz. fresh lime juice

¹/₄ oz. agave nectar

2 dashes of Angostura bitters

³/₄ oz. pineapple juice

Place all of the ingredients in a cocktail shaker filled with ice and shake until chilled.

Strain into an Old Fashioned glass filled with ice.

FINISHING TOUCHES
Garnish with two pineapple leaves.

GAMORA'S ZOMBIE

This cocktail is Marlo's take on the classic Zombie, using a bespoke spice mixture to keep up with the complexity provided by the mixture of rums. This fantastical cocktail, and its artful skull-shaped vessel, stir the imagination.

Marlo Gamora, bartender at Dante NYC and Mother of Pearl, New York

1 oz. Barbados rum

1 oz. Jamaican rum

¼ oz. Marlo's mix

¾ oz. passion fruit syrup

¾ oz. ruby red grapefruit juice

¾ oz. fresh lime juice

¼ oz. absinthe

1 oz. 151-proof demerara rum

Place all of the ingredients, except for the 151-proof rum, in a blender and pulse to combine.

Pour it into a skull-shaped mug filled with fresh pebble ice and top with the 151-proof rum.

FINISHING TOUCHES
A skull mug is recommended by the mixologist, but any spooky, Halloween-themed mug will do the trick. Place the cocktail in a bowl containing dry ice and garnish with mint, a brandy-soaked cherry, a lime wheel, a cocktail umbrella, and an orange peel flower (see page 77). If desired, you can also mist with absinthe for an added aromatic element.

For Marlo's mix: Combine equal parts cinnamon syrup (see page 237) and St. Elizabeth Allspice Dram.

BELLA SOCO

According to Jelani, "This cocktail takes the classic idea of a flaming tiki drink and pushes it one step further. It is a mysterious red color with a bubbling red rock in the middle of it. The pretty bouquet of fruit slices and orchids around it acts as both a garnish and a barrier for the guest to sip behind while allowing the flame to seemingly burn forever. A lot of people are curious about the volcano lime garnish and I always tell them that it is an 'ancient tiki secret.'"

Jelani Johnson, bartender at Clover Club, New York

1½ oz. Yaguara Cachaça

½ oz. El Dorado 15-Year-Old rum

¼ oz. Hamilton 151 Overproof Demerara Rum

1½ oz. Don's mix

¾ oz. fresh lime juice

¼ oz. simple syrup

dash of Angostura bitters

Place all of the ingredients in a cocktail shaker containing 2 ice cubes and shake vigorously.

Strain into a snifter and top with crushed ice.

FINISHING TOUCHES

Garnish with a grapefruit slice, a lime wheel, an orchid blossom, and a volcano lime. To make the volcano lime, place a sugar cube in a spent lime half. Fill the shell with Hamilton 151 Overproof Demerara Rum that has been colored with red food dye. Light the sugar cube on fire and grate some cinnamon over it to release the aromatics and create sparks. Place in the center of the drink and hem it in with the other garnishes so that you can imbibe in safety.

For Don's mix: Combine 2 parts grapefruit juice and 1 part cinnamon syrup (see page 237).

FEISTY MEISTER

This drink requires passion and flame—and a bit of caution.

Courtesy of Honeycut, Los Angeles

1 oz. Jägermeister

1/2 oz. blended Jamaican rum

1/2 oz. 5-year-old Barbados rum

1/2 oz. orange juice

1/2 oz. fresh lime juice

1/2 oz. passion fruit syrup

1/2 oz. Orgeat (see page 207)

Place all of the ingredients in a blender and pulse until combined.

Pour into a Collins glass filled with crushed ice.

FINISHING TOUCHES

Place a spent lime half, fruit facing up, on top of the crushed ice. Fill the lime with 151-proof rum and light the liquor on fire. Sprinkle cinnamon onto the flame to create sparks. Wait until the fire has gone out before consuming.

ACKNOWLEDGMENTS

I've been equally fascinated and charmed by the glamour of stimulating spirits as far back as I can remember. Attending Sunday mass as a toddler and held aloft by my father to get a better view during the Consecration, I clapped and sang out while the priest held the glistening, golden chalice high over his head, exclaiming in a clear declarative voice: "God. Drinks. Beer!"

Researching and writing this book was a joy—almost as much as that exalted first golden chalice experience. Hands down, there's no better publisher to work with than the Cider Mill team—total professionals.

I thank my husband, Bill, who is always there for me: through research, writing, photo shoots, and, yes, enduring construction of our home speakeasy. I thank Bill and my mother, Virginia, for taste-tasting so many of my creations as well as for their input.

I thank Jessica Wohlers, an artful polymath (photography, painting, styling, and mixology to name a few) not to mention being a spectacular niece, too. Jessica introduced me to so many talented mixologists from Manhattan and Brooklyn. I also especially thank Macchu Pisco's Melanie and Lizzie Asher—and cousin Natasha—for the very enthusiastic love and support from New York to Miami, London, and Peru. I thank these extraordinary, successful women for their time and insight.

I thank Joe Gallo, a public relations professional who went the extra mile to provide recipes, photos, and introductions to the top-shelf brands he represents.

And I raise my glass in salute to all the featured mixologists—their creativity and dedication is exceptional, breathtaking, and delicious.

I pay a special tribute to my father, George, who left me with a meadow of memories that continue to spark our garden-to-glass happy hours.

Cheers to life everlasting!

INDEX

ABOUT
CIDER MILL PRESS

Good ideas ripen with time. From seed to harvest,
Cider Mill Press brings fine reading, information, and entertainment
together between the covers of its creatively crafted books.
Our Cider Mill bears fruit twice a year, publishing
a new crop of titles each spring and fall.

"Where Good Books Are Ready for Press."

Visit us on the Web at
www.cidermillpress.com
or write to us at
12 Spring Street
PO Box 454
Kennebunkport, Maine 04046

ABOUT THE AUTHOR

Leeann Lavin writes a food and drink column for Examiner.com about the New York food and drink world. She owns the popular Garden Glamour blog, covering the nexus of garden art and culinary art. She is also the author of *The Hamptons & Long Island Homegrown Cookbook* and a contributing author to Savoring Gotham. A 2015 IACP Cookbook judge, Lavin is also a BlogHer Influencer and a SheKnows Expert.

IMAGE CREDITS

Pages 7, 23, 28, 31, 44, 47-48, 89, 92, 138, 158, 174, 181, 192, 197, 211, 218, 236, 239, and 247 courtesy of Doug Young; pages 27, 86, 90-91, 118-119, 173, and 216 courtesy of Hennessy; pages 32, 35, and 95 courtesy of Jessica Wohlers; pages 38-39 courtesy of Chandon; pages 40, 50-51, 84, 96, 112, 132, 177, 208, and 212 courtesy of Leeann Lavin; page 131 courtesy of Isaac Morrison; pages 59, 116, and 222 courtesy of Tom Sebazco; pages 83, 126, 165, 198, 215, and 232 courtesy of Josh Suchan; page 133 courtesy of Fabio Latham; page 145 courtesy of Ryan Liloia; pages 157 and 161 courtesy of Calum O'Flynn; pages 231, 248 (top right) Thomas Schauer, courtesy of Xavier Herit; page 244 courtesy of Jelani Johnson.

All other photos are used under official license from Shutterstock.com.